DREAM
INTERPRETATION
MADE SIMPLE

DREAM INTERPRETATION
MADE SIMPLE

Praying Medic

INKITY
PRESS™

Inkity Press™
137 East Elliot Road, #2292, Gilbert, AZ 85299

This book and other Inkity Press titles can be found at:
InkityPress.com and PrayingMedic.com

Available from IngramSpark.com, and various retail outlets.

For more information visit our website at **www.inkitypress.com**
or email us at **admin@inkitypress.com** or **admin@prayingmedic.com**

ISBN-13: 978-1-947968-08-0 (Inkity Press)

Printed in the U.S.A.

To TWO FRIENDS WHO TAUGHT me the value of dreams and inspired me to pursue a greater understanding of them—Paula Otano and Melody Paasch.

As a former atheist and someone who had not had a dream in 25 years, I have unique qualifications to teach others about dreams. For most of my life, I was an atheist and had no dreams and therefore no interest in the subject. But in 2008, dreams came to me regularly, sometimes as many as ten dreams per night. I've studied dreams extensively since then and teach others what I've learned. Whether you consider yourself to be spiritual, devoutly religious, or agnostic, I hope you'll consider joining me in a journey to discover where dreams come from and what they mean.

Dreams are an intensely personal matter. The secret issues of life, our flaws and weaknesses, as well as our strengths are revealed in them. If you want to learn the deep issues of a person's life, ask them to tell you their dreams. You'll learn things about your friends they aren't aware of themselves. This book contains dozens of dreams I've had over more than a decade, as well as dreams shared by friends and acquaintances.

Because dreams are by nature, intensely personal, you'll learn more about me in this book than any book I've written. I discuss subjects

I've never spoken about publicly. Even my best friends aren't aware of some of the personal matters you'll discover in this book. You'll see the good and the bad in me. That's a risk some authors would not take, but I'm allowing you into the private areas of my life because I believe that as you observe how I handle my dreams, it will help you gain a better perspective of yours.

This book is divided into four sections. The first section looks at the origin of dreams. Section two provides examples of different types of dreams and explains how they are interpreted. Section three provides practical tips on applying dreams in your everyday life. The last section contains a dictionary of common dream symbols.

~ Praying Medic

Part One

CHAPTER ONE

The Origin of Dreams

FOR MILLENNIA, MANKIND HAS ASKED, Where do dreams come from? The way in which we answer this question will determine the meaning we assign to dreams. Two dominant views exist about the origin and meaning of dreams. The field of psychology asserts that man is a two-part being. Our physical body is controlled by our mind, and dreams originate in our soul. There is no agreement on what the soul is, where it is located, if it is a physiological part of our body, or how it operates. At present, the best guess is that our soul controls the abstract concepts of thought, will, and emotion. Scientists theorize that dreams originate in the soul because they tend to be illogical. Logical function resides in the brain. Dreams, therefore, must be manifestations of the soul.

Psychologists like Sigmund Freud once thought dreams expressed our unconscious desires and motivations. Recent theories suggest that they're hallucinations. Secularists claim dreams have no real meaning, and when one seems to predict a future event, it's attributed to coincidence. I've had many dreams in recent years that foreshadowed future events. The idea that they would *all* be coincidental seems far-fetched.

The other dominant view of dreams comes from the Judeo-Christian perspective. The Bible teaches that man is a three-part being. We are a spirit; we have a soul, and we inhabit a physical body.

The Bible suggests dreams are a form of communication from God.

> *For God may speak in one way, or in another,*
> *Yet man does not perceive it.*
> *In a dream, in a vision of the night,*
> *When deep sleep falls upon men,*
> *While slumbering on their beds,*
> *Then He opens the ears of men,*
> *And seals their instruction.*
> JOB 33:14-16

If dreams are a form of spiritual communication, it may be helpful to have a basic understanding of spiritual mechanics. Next, I'll briefly describe how the spiritual body operates. The spiritual body is composed of spiritual light that is not perceived by the human eye. This is why angels are invisible until and unless they manifest in a physical body. The spiritual body does not rely on the structures of the physical body for communication. It has an analogous set of spiritual senses. When we see a spirit being, we don't see them with our physical eyes. When we hear an angel speak, the sound is not created by a being with physical vocal cords. Spirits do not have eardrums, retinas, or optic nerves. Spiritual communication is done primarily through the transmission of thought impressions and visual imagery directly from spirit-to-spirit, bypassing the body's physical structures.

Have you ever noticed that in dreams, you know certain facts without ever being told them? You know your brother will get a new job. You know the car in front of you will go through a red light. You know your boss is embezzling money. No one had to tell you these things. You know them, just as surely as you know your name. We know things in dreams without being told them because spiritual information is not communicated through speech, but through thoughts—directly to our spirit.

The human brain processes input from the physical senses of touch, taste, sight, smell, and sound, but it also receives information from the spiritual senses. Our brain is conditioned to prioritize information from the physical world. When information from the spiritual world is received, we have difficulty interpreting it outside the context of the physical world. This is one reason why dreams are difficult to understand, but there is another issue to consider. The brain has difficulty making sense of spiritual information because it is of a different *nature* than intellectual information. Spiritual knowledge is information of a different order. Allow me to illustrate this difference.

The brain can make sense of the emotion our soul produces called *grief* when it is connected to the intellectual context of a situation called *death*. In this case, the brain's cognitive center receives a message of death and the soul attaches the emotion of grief to it. The emotion and the intellect agree. The brain can likewise understand the emotion called *joy* when the cognitive setting is a wedding. Again, there is emotional and intellectual agreement. This is how the soul and brain—emotion and intellect—normally operate. But in dreams, we're just as likely to feel joy when someone dies or grief at a friend's wedding. Dreams create emotional and intellectual disagreement.

The fact that an emotion is felt in a dream does not necessarily mean it is created in the soul. If the soul were to create an emotion, it would likely correspond to an appropriate event. The fact that in a dream, the emotion is connected to an *inappropriate* event suggests that emotion and event are joined by some other mechanism. That other mechanism is our spirit. Like the soul, the spirit receives and transmits emotions but it does so for a completely different purpose.

Our spirit sends and receives messages that have *symbolic* rather than *literal* (logical) meaning. Spiritual messages are not about what they seem to be. Our brain doesn't understand them because they're symbolic and must be decoded. Our soul doesn't understand them because it did not create them. Dreams are an enigma to the soul and body because they are manifestations of our spirit.

Some dreams *do* originate in the soul. These dreams, like a poorly written tale, have no point. Because they're not spiritual, they're not symbolic, and the dreamer typically doesn't feel a strong emotion. Soul dreams are devoid of the encouragement, instruction, warning or other features found in spiritual dreams.

Although most dreams are spiritual in nature, they are not created by our spirit. They're created and sent by other spirit beings. Some spirits act as messengers. Under the right circumstances, our spirit receives them. (The circumstances for receiving them will be discussed shortly.) Dreams may come from both good and evil spirits. What do I mean by an "evil spirit?"

We all do bad things at times. When we do, we usually feel regret and try not to repeat the bad behavior. But some people enjoy hurting others. They inflict pain intentionally, and take pleasure in doing it. This is the behavior of an evil spirit.

Dreams from evil spirits tend to be dark and filled with muted colors. The dreamer usually feels negative emotions like fear, guilt, shame, lust, or rejection. The subject matter of these dreams tends to be something evil. Here's an example of a dream from an evil spirit:

One night, I had a dream of going with my wife to a job interview in a high-rise building. As we got in the elevator, I spoke to a man. During the conversation, I became angry and yelled at him. Immediately afterward, I felt ashamed. I then became concerned that my wife's potential employer may have been in the elevator. When the elevator door opened, I wandered around looking for the right office. I went from room to room but quickly became lost, and felt confused. A woman wearing all black clothing escorted me to an office. I noticed that her eyes were black, and her makeup was unusually dark. She seemed overly serious for the occasion and even a little threatening. I went into the room she led me to and sat at a table. My wife was already there. Her potential employer ignored me. He ordered breakfast for himself and my wife, Denise, and helped her cut her food but took no notice of me.

The first emotion I felt in the dream was anger. The second was shame. Then I felt worried. Next came confusion. When I met the woman,

I felt threatened. When I met the potential employer, he ignored me. I felt unimportant, and then jealous. The negative emotions I felt in the dream suggest that it was sent by an evil spirit. The austere woman in black clothing and dark makeup confirmed that it was from an evil spirit. When someone in black attire appears in a dream, they often turn out to be an agent of the enemy. Dreams from evil spirits are designed to cause fear, discouragement, lust, shame or some other negative emotion. They are not enjoyable, but we do have some control over the dreams we receive. That subject will be discussed shortly.

CHAPTER TWO

The Purpose of Dreams

GOD DESCRIBES HIMSELF AS THE ruler of a spiritual kingdom. It is referred to in the gospels as the kingdom of God. This kingdom is governmental in nature. Jesus illustrated its attributes in parables. Today, God's Spirit reveals them through the parabolic imagery of dreams.

One night, I had a dream about the kingdom of God. In it, I watched as various people experienced the kingdom. The first man I saw was a drug addict and petty criminal. He kept an eye out for the police who might catch him doing something wrong. He lived to have his desires met. His was a life of fear, selfishness, and using others. Then he entered the kingdom of God.

I saw him dressed in a uniform sitting on a stool at the opening in a wall. The wall was a divider between a prison cell and the kingdom of God. The gap in the wall was a gate about four feet wide, which he guarded. I watched him get up and walk around in the kingdom, which was an endless expanse as far as the eye could see. As he explored this new place, he looked for familiar things but found nothing like what he experienced in the world. There was no crime, no drugs, and no police. He didn't fear being caught committing a crime because no crimes happened in the kingdom. All his needs were met, and he was filled with peace.

Then he met God, the Father, who had only good things to say about him. The Father provided everything he needed. He went back to the stool and sat at the gate. His new job was telling those who asked how they could enter the kingdom. This experience profoundly changed the way in which he lived in the world. Although his problems didn't immediately disappear, he lived from the reality he experienced in the kingdom. The freedom he felt there allowed him to live free; he never lived in fear again.

I was also in the dream. In the world, I looked for acceptance and wanted to be understood. Once I entered the kingdom, I found acceptance and everyone seemed to understand me. Even more amazing was that they liked me. In the dream, I realized I had no enemies. When I met God, the Father, I encountered absolute acceptance and love. I was the apple of His eye. I left God's kingdom and went back into the world, and the experience changed how I lived. I no longer sought acceptance. I lived from the reality I had experienced in the kingdom and never again wondered if I was good enough.

A third person appeared in the dream who feared he would never have enough money. Although he had a good job, and invested his money wisely, he lived with a nagging fear of poverty.

In the kingdom, he traveled from place to place and noticed that no one worried about money. In fact, there were no worries of any kind. People had piles of cash. He found that he could easily get as much money as he wanted from any stranger. No one cared how much they had or how much they gave away. There was abundance for everyone. This man returned to the world, and the experience changed the way in which he lived. Experiencing heaven's provision and knowing that God's economy never lacked resources gave him a freedom with money he never thought possible. His fear of poverty vanished. He lived in the world from the reality he experienced in the kingdom and gave abundantly to others.

The theme of this dream was God's abundant love, acceptance, and provision. His kingdom is perfection. Once you experience it, you can live in this world from the realities you experience there.

Dreams show us a different reality. In them, God reveals truths of which we are unaware. We're given a chance to observe ourselves in a spiritual mirror in the hope that we might believe what we see and ask God how we might live differently.

CHAPTER THREE

Dream, Vision, Visitation or Something Else?

NOT ALL SPIRITUAL EXPERIENCES WE have at night are dreams. In this chapter, we'll examine these experiences and explain their purpose.

After Jesus was born in Bethlehem, he received gifts from the Magi. King Herod asked them in secret to bring the child to him. They went to Bethlehem but decided not to honor Herod's request after being warned in a dream:

> *Then, being divinely warned in a dream that they should not return to Herod, they departed for their own country another way.*
> MATT 2:12

We don't know exactly how the message was delivered to the Magi or what was said, but apparently, the warning came the way most dreams do. Compare that account to the next verse in Matthew's gospel.

> *Now when they had departed, behold, an angel of the Lord appeared to Joseph in a dream, saying, "Arise, take the young Child and His mother, flee to Egypt, and stay there until I bring you word; for Herod will seek the young Child to destroy Him."*
> MATT 2:13

Matthew called Joseph's experience a dream, but also noted that an angel appeared to him and gave him the message. When a heavenly messenger visits us in person, rather than being a simple dream, the experience is called a *visitation*.

Compare those two experiences with this one:

> *Now when they had gone through Phrygia and the region of Galatia, they were forbidden by the Holy Spirit to preach the word in Asia. After they had come to Mysia, they tried to go into Bithynia, but the Spirit did not permit them. So passing by Mysia, they came down to Troas. And a vision appeared to Paul in the night. A man of Macedonia stood and pleaded with him, saying, "Come over to Macedonia and help us." Now after he had seen the vision, immediately we sought to go to Macedonia, concluding that the Lord had called us to preach the gospel to them.*
> ACTS 16:6-10

The Apostle Paul sought the right place to preach the gospel. The Holy Spirit revealed the correct location in a night vision. In a night vision, the individual is awake and the scene plays out as it would in a dream.

I have, on three occasions, received a combination of ten dreams and visions in a single night. In August of 2008, I received the following night visions (a few have been omitted to preserve the privacy of the individuals involved). In the first vision, I was with my wife. We encouraged a friend to persist through a present situation and be patient as he waited for God's timing. We told him to go into a room, close the door and pray, and remain in there until God did what He needed to do. In the next vision, I was with my wife and a friend named Mike. We helped him sense the presence of God. In the vision that followed, I shared my spiritual journey with Mike. In the next one, I saw myself praying for him to receive prophetic visions and dreams. In the next vision, I showed him my prophetic journal. I was awake during all of these visions and saw the events play out like scenes before me. After each one ended, I tried to go back to sleep, and that's when the next vision began.

Angelic Visitations

The most common Greek word in the Bible for angel, ἄγγελος (angelos) can be defined as "messenger." The Bible is full of references to angels, that are often seen delivering messages to people who are scared half to death by their presence. As we've seen, angels can deliver messages in dreams. I've had many experiences at night where I heard a voice speak a simple message. My wife has had them, too. One night, she heard a voice say, "Beware of those who are called, but not chosen." On a couple of occasions, we received nearly identical messages a few days apart. These messages are delivered by the voice of an unseen messenger. Although we don't see them, the Bible supports the idea that they are angels. Why would a message be delivered by the voice of an angel instead of a dream? It could be that some messages are important enough to God that He doesn't want to risk an incorrect interpretation. To make sure we receive the right message, He sends an angel to deliver the exact words.

A Visitation from Jesus

On September 3, 2008, while living near Olympia, Washington, I awoke in the night to the sound of music, but I saw no images around me. I then heard a voice speaking that delivered the following message. "I will pour out my Spirit says the Lord. I will visit Olympia in fifteen months. I, the Lord will raise up Olympia in fifteen months."

I wrote down the words and noted that my digital clock showed the time of 3:21.

As I tried to go back to sleep, the voice returned. Again, I heard sound, but saw no images. I heard Kim Clement leading worship with a congregation. He sang the song "Sacrifice is Beautiful." The same voice that delivered the first message spoke again: "Do not leave. Stay where you are. In fifteen months, it will come to pass."

I wrote down the second message, then tried to go back to sleep, but a few minutes later, the voice returned with a final message: "I am giving you a key, do not lose it!"

I was awake, so it would not be considered a dream. I saw nothing during the experience, so it would not be called a vision. The sender of the message claimed to be the Lord, which would classify it as a visitation. In the last message, the Lord said I was being given a key. I didn't receive an *actual* key that night. The key would therefore be symbolic. What might it represent? A key unlocks doors. There are a few generic references to keys in the Bible, but a special key—the key of David—is mentioned in Isaiah 22:22, and again in Revelation 3:7. Jesus also referred to the keys of the kingdom in Matthew 16:19. These keys refer to the authority granted to someone to open and shut the doors of the kingdom. Of what kind of authority does this speak?

I lived near Olympia, Washington, when I had this experience. Jesus gave me a key which represents authority I had been granted. He mentioned the city of Olympia twice. From this, I would conclude that some believers are given authority that can be exercised over a geographic region. His instruction to remain in Olympia seems to confirm that the authority was regional.

Visitations from the Cloud of Witnesses

There are reasons for caution regarding visitations from the souls of the departed. Let's examine what the Bible says on this matter. A helpful account is found in Matthew's description of the transfiguration of Jesus.

> *"Now after six days Jesus took Peter, James, and John his brother, led them up on a high mountain by themselves; and He was transfigured before them. His face shone like the sun, and His clothes became as white as the light. And behold, Moses and Elijah appeared to them, talking with Him."*
> MATT 17:1-3

The book of Deuteronomy instructs us not to communicate with the the spirits of the dead (see Deut 18:10-11), yet here was Jesus talking with two saints who had been dead for centuries. We must now ask if Jesus violated God's prohibition. The Bible says Jesus lived a sinless life, so we know it was not a violation of God's law for him to speak with Moses and Elijah.

The writer of the book of Hebrews had much to say about those who had passed into eternity. He referred to them as "the cloud of witnesses." Hebrews chapter 11 is sometimes referred to as the "hall of faith." The writer waxes eloquently about how—by faith—the patriarchs, the prophets, and lesser-known people pleased God. The last two verses of the chapter summarize his point:

> *"And all these, having obtained a good testimony through faith, did not receive the promise, God having provided something better for us, that they should not be made perfect apart from us."*
> HEB 11:39-40

The writer of the book of Hebrews noted that the gathering of saints who had preceded us in death would not be perfect or *complete* without us. We must be joined to them in order to have a complete body. Chapter 12 begins:

> *"... since we are surrounded by so great a cloud of witnesses..."*

The phrase in this verse, *are surrounded by*, means "to be closely joined to a person or thing." It speaks of our relationship to the cloud of witnesses. The writer implied that the spirits of the departed surround us; we are in their midst. We *presently* have an intimate relationship with those who have run their race well. If you're wondering what a *saint* is, allow me to explain this term.

Catholicism teaches that a follower of Jesus must accomplish a number of great things and be recognized by the Vatican to be a saint. The New Testament, and in particular, the teachings of the Apostle Paul, say otherwise. In many of his letters, Paul addressed ordinary believers as saints. Whether living in a physical body or in eternity, any believer may be referred to as a saint.

I suspect that in some cases when we meet someone in a dream, it is not an image of them we're interacting with, but the spirit of that person. Some time ago, I ran across a rare audio recording of a message by C.S. Lewis. The speech formed the outline of what would become one of his most well-known books—*Mere Christianity*. I converted the audio message into a video and posted it on YouTube. The project took most of the day. As I worked, I thought about this beloved saint whose writings have inspired a generation. I admire gifted writers. I draw inspiration from them, pick up tips and learn from their examples. Lewis is the person by whom I gauge my own writing, and at times, my own thinking. No one wrote as eloquently or as intelligently about the issues of modern society.

I never met Lewis. He joined the great cloud of witnesses in 1963. When I created the video, I spent an entire day wondering about him and reflecting on how his life had affected mine. Time seemed to stand still that afternoon. And then I went to sleep.

That night, I had a dream where Lewis visited me. I did not see him the way you typically see someone in a dream. It's not as though we sat at a table talking. I knew I was in his presence, the way you know certain things in dreams. I did not hear him speak in that distinctive accent. He spoke to me spirit-to-spirit through thoughts. The purpose of our meeting was so that he could teach me about writing. There I was, being tutored by the spirit of one of my favorite men, and what he shared was surprisingly practical.

He explained how the proper selection of words is critical to a writer's success. He illustrated his point with problems he had encountered by choosing the wrong words in his own stories. He noted that our choice of words creates either a favorable or unfavorable impression in the mind of the reader. He gave examples of how the choice of this word or that one created a completely different set of circumstances. He advised me to choose my words with care.

Some would argue that this experience was the result of eating too much pizza. Some might say my mind was working out the issue I was focused on that day. Others would call it an evil spirit masquerading as Lewis. It may have been the Holy Spirit or Jesus teaching me through a persona with which I was familiar. And some would say it was indeed the spirit of Lewis who was given access to me that night so that he might assist me in advancing God's plans.

When these saints meet with us in dreams, they tend to help those who are engaged in endeavors similar to their own earthly calling. They usually share advice on how to avoid the problems they encountered during their time on earth. They give suggestions about how to accomplish things with expediency and efficiency, to shorten the learning curve. And that is exactly what Lewis did. Although I once opposed anything of this nature, meeting Lewis in this dream caused me to rethink my position.

On occasion, we may be allowed to visit with a saint who has departed. They usually have instruction from God as to how they might assist us. In my case, Lewis had the ability (and presumably, permission from God) to help with my divine assignment as a writer.

Unless the spirit we're communicating with has a divinely ordained purpose for the meeting, the enemy may have a purpose for it. This is why it can be dangerous for *us* to seek these relationships. If we initiate contact with a spirit, not knowing whether there is a divine purpose for it, we leave ourselves open to the influence of an evil spirit that is looking for just such an encounter.

One type of spirit of which to be wary is a familiar (or familial) spirit. These spirits have an attraction to certain families. They interact with a family's descendants over generations, often pretending to be the spirit of a departed relative. A familiar spirit wants to develop lasting relationships. They may ask us to trade something like knowledge or power in exchange for companionship. Over time, we may become dependent on them.

Familiar spirits may also have (or pretend to have) extensive knowledge of our family lineage. They can become violent or threatening when told to leave. True spirits of the departed don't put demands on the ones they visit. They tend to be concerned only with imparting joy or hope to one who may be grieving. They are not interested in developing lasting relationships.

Testing the Spirits

There is a misconception about the spirit world that says every spirit is fiercely loyal either to God or Satan, and it's our job to discern each spirit's loyalty. What we want is a litmus test that will settle the matter forever. Some believe such a test exists, and that it is found in the bible:

> *"By this you know the Spirit of God: Every spirit that confesses that Jesus Christ has come in the flesh is of God, and every spirit that does not confess that Jesus Christ has come in the flesh is not of God."*
> 1 JN 4:2-3

This verse has become a standardized test given to potential evil spirits. Simply ask a spirit if Jesus came in the flesh. If the answer is no, the spirit is evil. If the answer is yes, the spirit is good. Unfortunately, the matter is not that simple. This instruction must be placed in its historical context. John wrote to people who had been influenced by false teachers, and in particular—the teaching of Gnosticism. One gnostic doctrine is that the physical world is utterly corrupt and evil. Gnostics argued that God would never inhabit a fleshly body because all flesh is evil. If He were God, Jesus could not have come in the flesh, therefore, He must have been a spirit or phantom. John's instruction was addressed to anyone who had heard this teaching. If any teacher denied that Jesus came in the flesh, believers could know they were not sent from God—but were teaching the lies of Gnosticism.

Many people use this verse to determine if a spirit is from God or Satan. But do we really believe that saints and God's angels can only tell the truth, and fallen angels and demons can only lie? Some believe that when a spirit is shown to be dishonest, it will always be dishonest. When one is proven to be truthful, it will always be truthful. We simply note whether a spirit is truthful or dishonest and the matter is settled. The scriptures, however, portray this issue differently as the following two stories illustrate:

A demon-possessed woman had followed the Apostle Paul and his friends for many days, loudly proclaiming, "These men are the servants of the Most High God, who proclaim to us the way of salvation!"

Does this sound like something an evil spirit would say? If this woman were to come into most churches, she'd be received as a prophet. She spoke the truth, even under the influence of a demon. Paul discerned the demon's presence and cast it out of her (see Acts 16:17-18).

The Lord instructed the prophet Isaiah to tell King Hezekiah the sickness he had contracted was fatal. The prophet delivered the message, but a short while later, God told him to go back and tell the King he would not die after all. Imagine Isaiah's confusion over being told the information he had just given was wrong.

These situations illustrate the true nature of the spiritual world. Demons can be honest. In the book of Job, Satan told the truth when God asked where he had been. Men of God can be wrong. There is a mixture of light and dark in all of us, and a litmus test won't reveal the truth. The best way to test the spirits—to see if something is of God—is the same way we test anything. Look at the fruit that comes from the experience.

How do we judge the fruit of an experience? Ask yourself how your time with this spirit has affected you. Has the encounter led you closer to God? Has it diverted your attention in any way away from Jesus and toward something else, even if that something else is not evil? Allow me to illustrate.

There is nothing wrong with getting to know your angels. But as you get to know them, you should also be increasing in your knowledge of God—the One they represent. If any spirit (or any human) causes you to focus more on angels and meeting with them than on meeting with God and getting to know Him better, you may want to re-evaluate where that relationship is taking you.

Although an evil spirit can tell the truth (as Legion did when Jesus demanded his name), they can't produce the fruit of the Spirit: love, joy, peace, long-suffering, kindness, goodness, faithfulness, gentleness, and self-control. Evil spirits can speak as ones who are wise. They can demonstrate great power, but the more you interact with them, the more you will bear the fruit of darkness and inevitably be lured away from the true light—Jesus. Any spirit you meet who does not help you grow closer to Him should be suspect.

Traveling in the Spirit

Have you ever had a dream where you visited a friend in their home? A few years ago, a friend of mine had injured his shoulder. One night, we had similar dreams. In my dream, I visited several friends. In his dream, I visited him at his home. In his dream, I sat beside him, sensed he had injured his shoulder and prayed for his healing. As I prayed, he felt something like a bolt of lightning pass through his body. When he awoke in the morning, he found that his injured shoulder was healed.

So, what happened?

Unlike our physical body, our spirit does not need sleep. My spirit traveled to his home while my body was asleep, and I prayed for his healing. I've had dozens of dreams where I've traveled somewhere to pray for a friend, given them a message, or encouraged them during a time of difficulty. Some of these may simply be dreams, but if the other person sensed that you visited them, consider the possibility that your spirit traveled there. If you're interested in learning more about this subject, I write about it in greater depth in my book *Traveling in the Spirit Made Simple.*

Part Two

CHAPTER FOUR

Recording Dreams

WHENEVER YOU RECEIVE A DREAM or heavenly message, the most important responsibility you have is recording it. Dreamers must become scribes. There are many ways to record your dreams. One friend keeps a computer on a table beside her bed. She records her dreams in a word processing document. A tablet or phone would serve the same purpose. Some prefer using a voice recorder. I have a stack of index cards, a pen, and a small flashlight on my nightstand. When I have a dream, I try to write it down immediately.

You may be tempted to interpret a dream before writing it down, particularly if it seems important, but you should resist the temptation. The risk of processing a dream mentally before writing it down is that you may fall back to sleep. If you do, you may never remember the dream, and since you didn't write it down, it may be lost forever. Always record your dreams as soon as possible.

I write my dreams on note cards and then transfer them to a word processing document. Each dream is dated, and a notation is made if it's a second or third dream for that date. Sometimes, I'll note what I was doing that day. The document becomes a searchable dream database which I can search by name or subject.

The document also serves as a spiritual journal. I record interpretations as well as dreams. This allows me to evaluate my interpretations over time and see if they are correct or if they need to be updated based on new information. I enter prophetic words I receive from others in my journal and important dreams that are sent to me.

Some people have dreams that are more like movies. Capturing every detail might keep you up all night, but it isn't necessary to record every detail. Begin by noting whether you are a participant or an observer. Briefly describe the scene, making note of any prominent buildings. Indicate who the main character is and briefly describe the action. Write down the name of anyone you know and any cities or street names. Record any prominent colors, especially the colors of vehicles. Note compass directions, numbers or Bible verses that are mentioned. Describe any emotions you feel. If a famous person or someone you admire appears, note their name and occupation. If you wake up and look at the clock, it may be helpful to note the time. (The relevance of these things will be explained shortly.)

An alternative to recording the intricate details of a dream is writing a summary of it. Some dreams lend themselves well to this method, particularly ones where an abstract concept is presented. (Conceptual dreams will be discussed in a later chapter.) If the details of a dream are hazy or difficult to describe, try capturing the essence of it in just a sentence or two. Occasionally, when summarizing a dream, the interpretation will come to you.

Revelation from God is like a river. It's going somewhere and, hopefully, taking you with it. Review your dreams regularly. Find out where they're going. I review my dreams about every three months. When I do, I always see a pattern developing that had escaped my awareness. These big picture views can help determine if you're on the right path or if you need a course correction.

CHAPTER FIVE

Principles of Dream Interpretation

I'M USING THE WORD "PRINCIPLES" in the title of this chapter for a reason. Dreams are best interpreted using a loose set of principles or guidelines rather than rules set in stone. Unlike engineering and physics, spiritual matters do not lend themselves well to formulas. Avoid the rigid application of any rule when it comes to interpretation. Dreams are communication between you and God. It's unwise to evaluate communication with your spouse by a set of rules and the same applies to dreams.

This book offers suggestions for dream interpretation, but it is not an exhaustive treatment of the subject and should not be considered the final authority. Use the tools provided and adapt their application as you see fit. Every dream element has more than one possible meaning. Dreams may have more than one correct interpretation and some interpretations will change over time.

Revelation from God may be understood and applied by using the mnemonic RIA. These letters stand for **R**evelation, **I**nterpretation, and **A**pplication.

Revelation is *what* God tells us. To capture the "what" of divine revelation, we should record the message somehow, lest we'll forget it. Recording revelation is separate from interpretation and application. As you record the essence of what God said, avoid the interpretative process. Do not try to determine what the dream means or how it applies to you. Doing so may cause you to add details that were not revealed. While those steps are essential, they have a proper place and time. The initial process of recording what God revealed should be done as objectively as possible without considering personal views. The one personal aspect to include would be any emotions you felt in a dream.

While our mind may retain a story for decades, it does not retain dreams for long. Dreams are quickly forgotten because they are not created in our soul. They're received and held in our spirit. While we sleep, our soul is passive, and our spirit takes control of our affairs. As we wake, our soul exerts more control, and our spirit becomes passive. Revelation or experiences with which our spirit was occupied while we slept soon fade from memory. Dreams must be recorded as soon as we wake before we are disturbed. If not, they will vanish with the day's activities. Even a brief conversation can erase the details of a dream forever.

Interpretation

Dreams and visions are spiritual messages. Spiritual messages are, in most cases, symbolic and they require interpretation. The process of interpretation is demonstrated in several passages in the Bible, which we'll look at next.

When King Nebuchadnezzar had a dream, he demanded not only that he be told the interpretation, but the dream itself. That story is found in Daniel chapter two.

> *Now in the second year of Nebuchadnezzar's reign, Nebuchad-*
> *nezzar had dreams; and his spirit was so troubled that his sleep*

left him. Then the king gave the command to call the magicians, the astrologers, the sorcerers, and the Chaldeans to tell the king his dreams. So they came and stood before the king. And the king said to them, "I have had a dream, and my spirit is anxious to know the dream."

Then the Chaldeans spoke to the king in Aramaic, "O king, live forever! Tell your servants the dream, and we will give the interpretation."

The king answered and said to the Chaldeans, "My decision is firm: if you do not make known the dream to me, and its interpretation, you shall be cut in pieces, and your houses shall be made an ash heap. However, if you tell the dream and its interpretation, you shall receive from me gifts, rewards, and great honor. Therefore, tell me the dream and its interpretation."

They answered again and said, "Let the king tell his servants the dream, and we will give its interpretation."

The king answered and said, "I know for certain that you would gain time, because you see that my decision is firm: if you do not make known the dream to me, there is only one decree for you! For you have agreed to speak lying and corrupt words before me till the time has changed. Therefore, tell me the dream, and I shall know that you can give me its interpretation."

The Chaldeans answered the king, and said, "There is not a man on earth who can tell the king's matter; therefore, no king, lord, or ruler has ever asked such things of any magician, astrologer, or Chaldean. It is a difficult thing that the king requests, and there is no other who can tell it to the king except the gods, whose dwelling is not with flesh."

For this reason, the king was angry and very furious, and gave the command to destroy all the wise men of Babylon. So the decree went out, and they began killing the wise men; and they sought Daniel and his companions, to kill them.

Then with counsel and wisdom Daniel answered Arioch, the captain of the king's guard, who had gone out to kill the wise men of Babylon; he answered and said to Arioch the king's captain, "Why is the decree from the king so urgent?" Then Arioch made the decision known to Daniel.

So Daniel went in and asked the king to give him time, that he might tell the king the interpretation. Then Daniel went to his house, and made the decision known to Hananiah, Mishael, and Azariah, his companions, that they might seek mercies from the God of heaven concerning this secret, so that Daniel and his companions might not perish with the rest of the wise men of Babylon. Then the secret was revealed to Daniel in a night vision. So Daniel blessed the God of heaven.

Daniel answered and said:
"Blessed be the name of God forever and ever,
For wisdom and might are His.
And He changes the times and the seasons;
He removes kings and raises up kings;
He gives wisdom to the wise
And knowledge to those who have understanding.
He reveals deep and secret things;
He knows what is in the darkness,
And light dwells with Him.
"I thank You and praise You,
O God of my fathers;
You have given me wisdom and might,
And have now made known to me what we asked of You,
For You have made known to us the king's demand."

Therefore, Daniel went to Arioch, whom the king had appointed to destroy the wise men of Babylon. He went and said thus to him: "Do not destroy the wise men of Babylon; take me before the king, and I will tell the king the interpretation."

Then Arioch quickly brought Daniel before the king, and said thus to him, "I have found a man of the captives of Judah, who will make known to the king the interpretation."

The king answered and said to Daniel, whose name was Belteshazzar, "Are you able to make known to me the dream which I have seen, and its interpretation?"

Daniel answered in the presence of the king, and said, "The secret which the king has demanded, the wise men, the astrologers, the magicians, and the soothsayers cannot declare to the king. But there is a God in heaven who reveals secrets, and He has made known to King Nebuchadnezzar what will be in the latter days. Your dream, and the visions of your head upon your bed, were these: As for you, O king, thoughts came to your mind while on your bed, about what would come to pass after this; and He who reveals secrets has made known to you what will be. But as for me, this secret has not been revealed to me because I have more wisdom than anyone living, but for our sakes who make known the interpretation to the king, and that you may know the thoughts of your heart.

"You, O king, were watching; and behold, a great image! This great image, whose splendor was excellent, stood before you; and its form was awesome. This image's head was of fine gold, its chest and arms of silver, its belly and thighs of bronze, its legs of iron, its feet partly of iron and partly of clay. You watched while a stone was cut out without hands, which struck the image on its feet of iron and clay, and broke them in pieces. Then the iron, the clay, the bronze, the silver, and the gold were crushed together, and became like chaff from the summer threshing floors; the wind carried them away so that no trace of them was found. And the stone that struck the image became a great mountain and filled the whole earth.

"This is the dream. Now we will tell the interpretation of it before the king. You, O king, are a king of kings. For the God of heaven has given you a kingdom, power, strength, and glory; and wherever the children of men dwell, or the beasts of the field and the birds of the heaven, He has given them into your hand, and has made you ruler over them all—you are this head of gold. But after you shall arise another kingdom inferior to yours; then another, a third kingdom of bronze, which shall rule over all the earth.

And the fourth kingdom shall be as strong as iron, inasmuch as iron breaks in pieces and shatters everything; and like iron that crushes, that kingdom will break in pieces and crush all the others. Whereas you saw the feet and toes, partly of potter's clay and partly of iron, the kingdom shall be divided; yet the strength of the iron shall be in it, just as you saw the iron mixed with ceramic clay. And as the toes of the feet were partly of iron and partly of clay, so the kingdom shall be partly strong and partly fragile. As you saw iron mixed with ceramic clay, they will mingle with the seed of men; but they will not adhere to one another, just as iron does not mix with clay. And in the days of these kings the God of heaven will set up a kingdom which shall never be destroyed; and the kingdom shall not be left to other people; it shall break in pieces and consume all these kingdoms, and it shall stand forever. Inasmuch as you saw that the stone was cut out of the mountain without hands, and that it broke in pieces the iron, the bronze, the clay, the silver, and the gold—the great God has made known to the king what will come to pass after this. The dream is certain, and its interpretation is sure."

Nebuchadnezzar's dream and its interpretation provide a panoramic view of the history of the world. Sequential kingdoms were described before a final, eternal kingdom was revealed. Note that each symbolic element was interpreted individually. A meaning was given for gold, silver, bronze, iron and clay. These meanings may apply to dreams we have. The King saw an impressive image. The stone that broke the image into pieces grew into a mountain. Daniel said the mountain represented God's enduring kingdom. Clues to the meaning of the stone are provided elsewhere in the Bible:

Jesus said to them, "Have you never read in the Scriptures: 'The stone which the builders rejected Has become the chief cornerstone. This was the Lord's doing, And it is marvelous in our eyes'?
MATT 21:42

Although Daniel was said to have skill in dream interpretation, he confessed that both dreams and their interpretations come from God. We receive messages from Him in the form of dreams or visions. Then, if we're able to hear His voice, He gives us the interpretations. Dreams are relational. Hearing God's voice is essential for their interpretation. Anyone can learn to hear God's voice with a little practice. My book *Hearing God's Voice Made Simple* provides practical instruction and exercises.

Daniel asked for time to receive Nebuchadnezzar's dream and its interpretation. He and his friends prayed, and God revealed the interpretation. The principle here is that interpretations are received through prayer.

Prayer is communicating with God; it's a two-way conversation. The way I communicate with Him is very natural. Most often, I'll ask what a dream means and wait for a thought to enter my mind that I had not yet considered. Because God's thoughts are not our thoughts, one way to know you've received a message from Him is when an idea comes to you that is different from the way you normally think. Those brilliant thoughts that pop into your head are not generally yours. They're from God, and they reveal His view of the matter. Interpretations can be given in a variety of ways. Typically, you'll receive a thought, seemingly out of nowhere, that answers the main questions related to a dream: who the dream is about, what it is about, and what it means.

When Denise and I discuss our dreams, God sometimes interrupts our conversation with an interpretation. She'll listen to me explain my latest dream, then boom! She'll blurt out an interpretation that neatly and precisely explains it.

The meaning of some items that appear in dreams can be found in the kingdom parables of the New Testament. In the following example, Jesus spoke a parable to His disciples and then explained its meaning:

On the same day Jesus went out of the house and sat by the sea. And great multitudes were gathered together to Him, so that He got into a boat and sat; and the whole multitude stood on the shore.

Then He spoke many things to them in parables, saying: "Behold, a sower went out to sow. And as he sowed, some seed fell by the wayside; and the birds came and devoured them. Some fell on stony places, where they did not have much earth; and they immediately sprang up because they had no depth of earth. But when the sun was up they were scorched, and because they had no root they withered away. And some fell among thorns, and the thorns sprang up and choked them. But others fell on good ground and yielded a crop: some a hundredfold, some sixty, some thirty. He who has ears to hear, let him hear!"

And the disciples came and said to Him, "Why do You speak to them in parables?"

He answered and said to them, "Because it has been given to you to know the mysteries of the kingdom of heaven, but to them it has not been given. For whoever has, to him more will be given, and he will have abundance; but whoever does not have, even what he has will be taken away from him. Therefore, I speak to them in parables, because seeing they do not see, and hearing they do not hear, nor do they understand. And in them the prophecy of Isaiah is fulfilled, which says:

'Hearing you will hear and shall not understand,
And seeing you will see and not perceive;
For the hearts of this people have grown dull.
Their ears are hard of hearing,
And their eyes they have closed,
Lest they should see with their eyes and hear with their ears,
Lest they should understand with their hearts and turn,
So that I should heal them.'

But blessed are your eyes for they see, and your ears for they hear; for assuredly, I say to you that many prophets and righteous men desired to see what you see, and did not see it, and to hear what you hear, and did not hear it.

Jesus then interpreted the parable for the disciples:

"Therefore, hear the parable of the sower: When anyone hears the word of the kingdom, and does not understand it, then the wicked one comes and snatches away what was sown in his heart. This is he who received seed by the wayside. But he who received the seed on stony places, this is he who hears the word and immediately

receives it with joy; yet he has no root in himself, but endures only for a while. For when tribulation or persecution arises because of the word, immediately he stumbles. Now he who received seed among the thorns is he who hears the word, and the cares of this world and the deceitfulness of riches choke the word, and he becomes unfruitful. But he who received seed on the good ground is he who hears the word and understands it, who indeed bears fruit and produces: some a hundredfold, some sixty, some thirty."

Note once again that each element is interpreted individually. A symbolic meaning is given for birds, seeds, thorns, hard ground, good soil, and the numbers 30, 60 and 100. The seed symbolized the "word of the kingdom" or the message that God loves us and wants us to be reconciled to Him. Birds that stole the seed represent evil spirits who negate the effect of the word in our hearts. The seeds that were sown on stony ground, by the wayside, and among thorns illustrate the conditions of people's hearts who reject God's message or allow its effect to be neutralized by the cares of the world. The good soil where the seed produced a harvest is the heart of a person who accepts God's message and allows it to change them. In the last line, Jesus said that in some, the word bears a thirtyfold return, in others, sixtyfold, and in others, one hundredfold. This provides one (but not the only) meaning for the numbers 30, 60, and 100.

When a subject is highlighted in a dream, look it up in a Bible dictionary. Read the passage(s) where it appears and see if one of the meanings given might apply to your dream. (A dictionary of symbolic terms is provided in chapter 22 of this book).

Application

When a dream provides direction, inspiration, warning, or encouragement, we must take steps to alter how we live based on what was revealed. This is application.

If you fail to correctly determine who or what a dream it is about, you will misapply it. Imagine that you have a wealthy father. In a dream, he gives you a new car as a birthday gift. In dreams, our father often represents God, the Father. Gifts speak of the spiritual gifts. Cars illustrate our ministry to others. God is likely saying He wants you to operate in a spiritual gift such as prophecy or healing. That is the interpretation of the dream. *Operating* in the gift is the application of it.

You might have a dream where you're traveling the world teaching about healing and miracles. Many people have dreams (or receive prophetic words) to this effect. But they mistakenly think God will sovereignly give them a new ministry without working for it. Their hope turns to disappointment when the new ministry never materializes.

To operate in healing and miracles, one must learn to release power and exercise authority. These skills can be learned but it takes practice. I spent hundreds of hours reading books, watching videos, and listening to podcasts on healing. I prayed for thousands of people. Once I had developed expertise on the subject, I then began teaching others. None of this happened automatically. When God gives us a dream about ministry, He shows us His desire, but it will remain unfulfilled if we don't put in the time and effort. When God gives us a dream about ministry, the *application* of the dream is the effort required to become competent.

Misconceptions exist about what exactly is considered *ministry*. Some teach that ministry is full time employment with a recognized church. According to the Bible, ministry is using our time and talents to serve others. We all minister to others in some capacity.

Dreams portraying natural disasters are common. In some cases, they're interpreted and applied literally. The dreamer then makes expensive and time-consuming preparations for a disaster that never comes. Correct application of a disaster dream can be tricky. Our application usually favors the things that most concern us. The intended application (from God's perspective) may be an issue we are unaware of when a dream is given, or God may have a different view of the future. Improper application happens in many cases because the dreamer's interpretation and application are influenced by fears, political beliefs, life circumstances, or their view of the future. Dreams are often misapplied because of confirmation bias. Most people have some idea of how they think the future will play out. Confirmation bias causes us to look for things that confirm what we believe to be true. When a dream is given, we tend to interpret it in a way that supports our personal views. Natural disaster dreams are seldom about natural disasters. Dreams about a foreign army literally invading our country may be symbolic of something else. But these dreams lend themselves to creating narratives of the future that we expect. Many times, these dreams are misinterpreted or misapplied. In other cases, the interpretation and application are correct but the time frame is misinterpreted.

Misapplication and misinterpretation can be avoided with practice. I keep a spiritual journal. Occasionally, I publish my dreams on my website or social media. This creates a public record and makes me accountable for interpretation and application. Tracking interpretation and application over time will reveal where you get it right and where you go wrong. I've often thought a dream applied to one issue, only to realize months or years later it applied to an entirely different matter. Misinterpretation and misapplication may result from having a closed mind. This will be discussed in a later chapter.

CHAPTER SIX

Literal versus Symbolic

Dreams that appear to be nonsense, when correctly interpreted, reveal profound truths. To uncover the message of a dream, we must know if it is intended to be taken literally or symbolically.

To determine which way a dream should be interpreted, first take an inventory of the main elements. Note those who are present. Identify any houses or vehicles. If you're driving a vehicle, where are you driving to, and where are you coming from? What route are you taking? Through what town? Is someone else driving? If so, who?

Generally, if a dream can be interpreted literally, it should be. Let's look at a couple of examples. I once had a dream where I was driving the car I owned at the time I had the dream. I was coming home from working at the ambulance service I worked for at that time, and I drove the route I normally drove. As I looked at the dashboard instruments, the temperature gauge indicated the engine was overheating. That was the content of the dream. Several days later, while driving that car home from work on the same route I saw in the dream, the timing belt failed. As a result, the water pump failed, and the engine overheated, ruining the cylinder head gasket.

Every element of the dream could be interpreted literally. I was driving the car I presently owned, on a road I normally drove, from a job I currently had. When all the elements of a dream can be interpreted literally, the entire dream should be interpreted literally. This was a warning dream. If I had taken the car to a mechanic, they would have recommended changing the timing belt, and I would have saved myself a lot of heartache and money.

If you have a dream where you're driving a car that you presently own, to the house where you presently live, from a job you currently have, but you are with a relative who died years ago, the dream *should not* be interpreted literally. Your relative could not *literally* be with you in the car today. If any element of the dream *cannot* be interpreted literally, the entire dream should be interpreted *symbolically*. Here's another example:

In 2011, my wife and I were renting a home in Washington state and were preparing to move to Arizona. Oddly, one morning we awoke after having the same dream. In both our dreams, we were sitting in the office of a title company, signing papers to close on a home loan.

A few months later, we moved to Arizona and found a house for sale that we wanted to buy. We made an offer, but there were problems. I took a fifty percent cut in pay when I transferred with my employer to Arizona. My wife became unemployed after the move. We had to qualify on my income alone, and that meant I had to work overtime to show the bank we could afford the mortgage payment.

There was also a problem with my hourly pay. My employer said they would increase my hourly pay, but they had not honored the agreement. At 4:30 pm on a Friday afternoon, I spoke with our human resource department, and learned that the general manager had not approved my raise because he was in the hospital. Payroll went out Monday morning. If my raise wasn't approved by then, my check the following Friday would be too small for us to qualify for the loan.

On Monday, I logged onto the company website out of curiosity to check my hourly pay rate. Much to my surprise, my raise went through over the weekend. I went to the human resource office and spoke with the same woman I had talked to on Friday. "Hello, I spoke with you on Friday about my raise."

"Oh, yes, I remember you."

"I checked the website this morning and was a little surprised to see it was approved."

"Really? I was under the impression it wouldn't be approved since the division general manager has to approve it, and he's been in the hospital. Let me take a look." She logged onto the website and checked. "Well, it seems you're right. The system shows that your raise was approved sometime Friday afternoon."

"But when I spoke to you on Friday afternoon, you said there's no way it could be approved until after the weekend."

"Yes, I remember saying that."

"I don't mean to sound ungrateful, but if the general manager was in the hospital and he couldn't approve my raise, who did?"

"I have no idea."

I wondered if maybe God sent an angel into the manager's office to approve my raise.

When the bank's underwriters looked at our tax returns, they discovered that my wife had a small business loss from the prior year, and they wanted an explanation. Also, my income—because it contained overtime—was in question. The underwriter contacted my employer several times and each time, my employer said something that made things worse.

One Friday afternoon, our loan officer gave us more bad news. "Hi, guys... It's been a pretty hectic week with underwriting. I was wondering if you guys believe in prayer."

My wife replied, "We've been praying ever since we made the offer. What going on?"

"You'll probably want to keep praying this weekend. You're going to need help if the loan is going to go through. We don't have a clear-cut answer yet. It could go either way. It's completely at the discretion of the underwriter."

I felt as though the dreams God had given us were a promise that we'd get the house. We went through frequent setbacks like this. Every time worry reared its head, we thought about the dreams and about what God had already done for us. He made a promise, and we knew He would keep it.

On Friday, the loan officer would call with bad news. We'd pray over the weekend. On Monday, he would call with good news. That's how it went almost every week. Despite the uncertainties, we gave notice that we were moving out of our apartment and scheduled movers to help us, though we didn't have official loan approval from the bank or a closing date.

One day, Denise received another call from the bank.

"Guys, we're coming down to the wire regarding your deposit money. There's a point in this process before which, if you withdraw your offer, or if you don't qualify for the loan, we can refund your earnest money. The time is approaching where you're going to lose your deposit if the loan doesn't go through. You have to make a choice. You can keep your offer on the table and hope you're approved and risk losing your deposit, or you can withdraw your offer."

The prospect of losing our earnest money frightened us. But I kept reminding Denise about the dream. We discussed withdrawing our offer, but decided to trust that God would make it happen. Denise explained to our loan officer, "We both had a dream on the same night that we were in an office signing papers to close on the loan. We're taking it as a promise from God that the loan will be approved, so we're keeping our offer on the table."

We had put down a cash deposit, but our closing money was invested in silver coins. God had given me several dreams in 2010 indicating that I should buy silver. At some point, we had to cash out the silver and deposit the money in escrow to cover closing costs. A few days before closing, we cashed out the silver. On the day we did, the spot price of silver was a little over $40 an ounce. Three days later, it had dropped to $28 an ounce. God allowed us to cash out our silver, doubling the value of our investment, just before the price dropped.

It was September 30th, 2011, the day we were supposed to close on the loan, but the bank had not yet given us an official closing date or time. We had to be out of our apartment that day and empty our storage units if we didn't want to pay for another month's rent. That morning, our loan officer called. "We're going to try to close late in the morning today."

We had scheduled the movers to pick up our furniture that morning, but now, we wouldn't be able to help direct them since we had to go to the title company to sign the papers for closing. We had our kids help the movers and got the manager to open our storage units. We instructed the movers to load up our belongings and meet us in a few hours at the new house. Hopefully, we'd have the keys.

It turned out we didn't get the keys. The seller of the house didn't show up at the signing, and our realtor couldn't reach them. Nobody knew where the keys were. So, we had movers on the clock, and they were just about to drop off our things, but we couldn't get in the house.

I had the movers unload our furniture in the driveway. Calls were made, and our realtor finally asked us to check inside the breaker panel outside the house. We looked, and sure enough, we found a key hidden there.

Buying the house was a stressful but divinely orchestrated ordeal. God remedied the problems. The crowning jewel came about a week later when we received a call from our loan officer. "I want to congratulate you two on pulling off one of the craziest home purchases I've ever witnessed. I also want to apologize for how we handled the closing. We dropped the ball on this one. I feel terrible about the trouble we put you through. The bank wants to show its appreciation for your business, so they've authorized me to make a donation on behalf of the bank, in the amount equal to one month's mortgage to the charity of our choice in your name, and you'll receive the tax credit for the donation. All I need is the payment information for the charity you want us to make the payment to." We were speechless. Who ever heard of a bank donating to a charity because they made a mistake? We gave the loan officer the name of a soup kitchen ministry run by a friend that operated on a shoestring budget. I called the man who ran the ministry and gave him the news. "I need to know who the bank should write the check to and their address." He was elated, but he had some news of his own.

"You're not going to believe this," he said.

"Try me."

"Yesterday, I was praying, and for some reason, I asked God to send someone from Arizona to help finance something He put on my heart. I wasn't even sure I knew anyone in Arizona. Today, you called with the answer to my prayer."

The ministry received the bank's donation, and we had a tax deduction that year, courtesy of the Chief Financial Officer of heaven.

The odds that my wife and I would have the same dream on the same night are incalculable. We were given the dreams to encourage us to stay the course when it seemed the cards were stacked against us. Often, literal dreams alert us to an opportunity that seems too good to be true. Other times, they're given to avert a catastrophe. Their literal nature is very directly intended to help us apply them correctly. Literal dreams require no interpretation, but applying them may require faith or courage.

I've recorded thousands of my own dreams and received thousands more from friends and acquaintances. It's surprising how few are intended to be interpreted literally. Most dreams are symbolic. God wants us to find the symbolic elements, decode them, then interpret and apply them correctly.

> *It is the glory of God to conceal a matter,*
> *But the glory of kings is to search out a matter.*
> PROV 25:2

CHAPTER SEVEN

Who is the Dream About?

FOR YEARS, MY WIFE HAS chided me because when I would tell her my latest dream, it would predictably begin with the words, "I was with a group of people..."

You might have a dream where every member of your family, church, or high school basketball team is present, but dreams are seldom about a group of people. Most often, they are about one person. But how do we determine who that person is?

A film may have a cast of thousands, but the story is told from the perspective of one character—the protagonist. Remove the protagonist from the cast, and the plot falls apart. In the same way, dreams tend to have one person as the main focus. If they're removed from the dream, there's no story to tell. The dream is about the person who plays the central role.

Although I have many dreams where I'm with a group of people, in almost every case, the dreams illustrate my role, responsibility, or ministry *to* that group of people. The dreams are not about the group. They're about *me*. Most of the dreams you have are about you.

Imagine having a dream where you're shopping for food with someone you believe to be your younger brother. He goes to the candy aisle and fills the shopping cart with candy bars, licorice, and other sweets. You put a loaf of bread in the cart, and he tosses it out. You pick it up and explain that he needs something other than candy. He looks at you with a confused expression, and the dream ends.

For the purpose of this discussion, let's assume that in real life, you don't have a younger brother. This indicates that the dream should be interpreted symbolically. Since dreams are usually spiritual in nature, your younger brother represents a person who is spiritually less mature than you. Bread represents spiritual nourishment. You're trying to give him spiritual food, but he doesn't want it. He prefers things that are spiritually unhealthy. The dream is about you. The subject is mentorship. Your task is to ask God who the symbolic brother is, what their problem is, and how you can help them.

Now let's imagine you have a dream with the same younger brother. In the dream, you're following him. You see him sitting at a bus stop crying. You watch him visit a hospital where he sits at the bedside of an older person with tears streaming down his face. In the next scene, he's at work. Although everyone around him is happy, he seems sad. The dream ends.

In this dream, you are not present. The dream is revealed from your brother's point of view; thus, the dream is about him. If, in this case, the brother was your actual brother, and if the older person was someone he knows, and the employer was his real employer, the dream could be interpreted literally. In this case, God is showing you the emotions he's currently experiencing (or will experience in the future). How you apply such a dream is up to you. You should certainly pray for him, but you may need to take on a counselor's role if he allows it. Most dreams are about one person. The perspective of the dream will usually reveal their identity.

When a famous person or someone you admire appears in a dream, the dream is seldom about them. In most cases, God is highlighting something about *them* that He wants to develop in *you*. If you see someone you admire operate in healing, God may be asking you to do the same. If they're teaching, God may be calling you to teach. I've had many dreams where I watched well-known healers and teachers in action. Although famous people were present, the dreams were not about them. God wanted me to know I have a similar calling. The dreams were about *me*. Before trying to contact someone you saw in a dream, consider the possibility that the dream is about you and not them. These dreams are usually intended to encourage you to pursue a similar calling or adopt an attitude similar to that of the person who appeared in the dream.

Even when you are not present in a dream, it may still be about you. Imagine having a dream where your city suffers a devastating earthquake. You are not present in the dream. You simply observe the destruction. Natural disaster dreams are usually meant to be interpreted symbolically. Earthquakes cause sudden, dramatic disruptions. Symbolically, they represent sudden, dramatic changes in life. An earthquake striking your city hits "close to home." The dream is likely to be about you. It may be a warning that changes are coming, and God wants you to be prepared.

Sometimes, the person or group referenced in a dream is given symbolically. Other times, they're portrayed plainly. Imagine a dream where, in the first scene, you see the U.S. Senate in session. In the second scene, you see a chessboard with chess pieces floating above it. Instead of black and white pieces, all the pieces are black. There are no rooks, knights, bishops, queens, or kings. You know by their size that all the pieces are pawns. Instead of being round, the pawns are square. As you observe them, they turn slowly, revealing two faces on each piece—a face on one side and a different face on the opposing side.

Now, lets identify the subject of this dream.

In dreams containing more than one scene, each scene has a different purpose. In general, the first scene establishes the subject matter for the *entire* dream. Regardless of the symbolic imagery found in the scenes that follow, all scenes in the dream usually pertain to, and should be interpreted in light of, the person or group shown in the first scene. This dream is about members of the Senate. Information about them is given in the second scene.

God often uses idioms, slang, and word pictures to convey meaning. What does it mean to be a "pawn?" The word *pawn* describes someone controlled or used by a person more powerful than them. A complete set of chess pieces contains both light and dark pieces, but in the dream, all the pieces were black. The color black often (though not always) symbolizes works of darkness. All the pieces had two faces. To be "two-faced" is to hold one set of values in private and another set in public or to be disloyal or dishonest. The dream suggests that members of the Senate are being used by people more powerful than themselves; they are aiding the kingdom of darkness, and are not being honest with the public. Determining who a dream is about can be confusing at first, but with practice you will be able to quickly identify them.

CHAPTER EIGHT

What is the Dream About?

CRUCIAL TO A DREAM'S INTERPRETATION is understanding its primary theme. While the person who is central to a dream is the one the dream is about, its action reveals its subject matter. Among the subjects illustrated in dreams are relationships, health, spiritual maturity, wisdom, divine protection, provision, our identity, divine destiny, and spiritual gifting.

Imagine having a dream where you're at a carnival, eating cotton candy while watching a thief pick the pockets of unsuspecting carnival-goers. Some would think this dream is a green light to go to the fair, but from God's perspective, it has nothing to do with a carnival. The care-free atmosphere of a carnival portrays the attitude of one who is unconcerned with matters of life and death, sin and redemption, heaven and hell. The thief is explained in John 10:10. *"The thief does not come except to steal, and to kill, and to destroy. I have come that they may have life, and that they may have it more abundantly."*

The dream suggests that the dreamer has been lulled into complacency while the enemy destroys the lives of unsuspecting victims all around him. How long will it be before the thief targets the dreamer?

One might ask why God conceals the real subject He intends to address in a dream. Most dreams discuss the serious issues of life. God uses symbolic imagery because we don't want to know what He thinks of our current situation. He tells us, but because most dreams are symbolic, we must work to understand the meaning. If we don't want to know, we can ignore our dreams and pretend He never shared His thoughts. God is a gentleman. He'll let us think He has no opinion if that is what we wish to think.

When our days on earth are done, and we step into eternity—the domain of the spirit—we'll find no taverns, no online shops, no video streaming sites, or hunting blogs. When we find ourselves in a miserable state, surrounded by people just as miserable as us, we may ask God why we weren't warned. He'll show us a highlight reel of all the dreams we were given that explained this world's realities—dreams we chose to ignore. But as we are now in the spiritual world, they'll make perfect sense, and we'll realize we were warned many times.

Imagine having a dream where thugs are chasing you. As you run from building to building trying to escape, you find locked doors and dead-end hallways. Then, out of the corner of your eye, you see a white building in the distance. You run toward it, and upon arriving, a door opens. You glance back and see your pursuers are still after you, so you duck inside the doorway. You follow a single, narrow corridor until it comes to a final section with no way out. At the end of the hallway, you notice a purple-colored chair like a throne. Knowing your pursuers will soon find you, but seeing no way out, you take a seat in the chair and resign yourself to whatever fate awaits you. The thugs smile as they approach. They're within arm's reach now, when suddenly, a trap door opens in the floor. They disappear, and the dream ends.

Dreams of being chased often portray a position of spiritual weakness or immaturity. Your enemy currently has an advantage over you; otherwise, you'd be pursuing them. You see a white building and move toward it. White often represents aspects of God's kingdom. You enter it (the kingdom) and find the way is straight and narrow (Matt 7:14). You see a purple chair. Purple represents royalty. Since you've entered God's kingdom, you've become part of the royal family of heaven. You take a seat, showing your acceptance of this relationship. Your enemy approaches, but just as they reach you, God pulls the lever on a trap door, and your enemies are rendered helpless. The dream illustrates several issues, but the main one is God's protection.

Now, let's consider a different kind of dream. In this one, you're in your childhood home. The scene is your bedroom. The toys you played with at that age and the bed you slept in are there. People you knew from childhood like siblings, aunts and uncles and your parents visit you. Each comes into your room for a few minutes, says something innocent, then leaves. Although nothing frightening happens in the dream, you feel terror. Then, the scene changes to the attic of that same house. You observe yourself in a metal cage being tormented by various monsters. Again, you feel only terror. The dream ends.

The fact that you're in the house you lived in as a child, that your bed and toys of that era are present, as well as people you knew at that time, means this dream is about you and the things you experienced at that age. Since the emotion felt in the dream is terror, something you experienced at that time was traumatic. In the first scene, all appears to be normal, suggesting that you currently have no memory of a traumatic childhood. But the attic scene provides information suggesting that the traumatic event(s) did happen.

It is common for adults to have amnesia of childhood trauma. The larger the gap in your childhood memories, the more likely you are to have suffered traumatic events of which you are unaware. God often gives these dreams to indicate a need for emotional healing. Except in cases of severe trauma, the healing process is simple and straightforward. I explain it in my book *Emotional Healing in 3 Easy Steps*.

God may address virtually any subject in a dream. He may speak to an issue of which we are unaware, or one we consciously understand, but refuse to address. In His own gentle way, He encourages us to take these matters seriously, accept His protection or healing, and walk in heavenly wisdom.

CHAPTER NINE

Dream Language

When God speaks to us in dreams, He establishes a set of relevant issues and uses a unique language. Our dream language is an environment and set of symbols that represent a world familiar to us. When my daughter was younger, she was a swimmer. Most of her dreams had a pool as the backdrop. My wife worked for many years as a graphic designer. Her dreams often featured computers. Now that she is pursuing a career as a painter, the setting of her dreams is her studio. Your dream setting and language will be familiar to you. I can't describe the unique dream language of thousands of people, but I can provide general principles to help you identify your dream language.

Each of us has a particular environment with which we are familiar. This environment is usually related to our occupation and may include certain buildings, rooms, people, activities, machines, modes of transportation, cities we visit, and other aspects of our vocation. Those who are not employed outside their home still have an environment with which they are familiar. They have a daily routine, people they know, and regular tasks they perform. God speaks to us through scenes and events that are familiar to us, but not to others.

I'm not a plumber. If God showed me a scene from a construction site familiar to a plumber, I would not understand how certain tools would be used or what they might represent, symbolically. For years, I worked as a paramedic. Many of my dreams take place in the setting of emergency medicine. Here's an example of the kind of dreams I have: In 2015, I had a dream where I cared for a number of patients with the same medical condition. Each patient had pink fluid in a container that was somehow attached to their body. I was supposed to monitor this fluid though I didn't know what it was or how it was to be monitored. I felt uncertain about how to take care of these patients. I did the best I could to make sure nothing bad happened to them while they were in my care. At the end of the dream, I was given an award for providing excellent care.

This dream confused me. Why would I receive an award for providing excellent care when I had no clue what was wrong with my patients or how I was supposed to monitor them? Later that day, it dawned on me what God was saying. I had made the observation the day I had the dream that many people have more knowledge of divine healing than me. Yet, I wrote a popular book on the subject.

It doesn't matter to God if we have exhaustive knowledge of a subject. What matters is that we do the best we can with the information and talent we have. In the dream, I had a poor understanding of my patient's condition, so my strategy was to prevent anything bad from happening to them. Not the most brilliant plan, but it got the job done. If we use the resources and knowledge God gives us, He'll fill in the gaps. Excellence is not perfection. Perfection is doing everything exactly right. No one is perfect, and many people beat themselves up over their imperfections. Perfection is the devil's substitute for excellence, which is doing the best we can, given the circumstances.

I would not expect you to have this kind of dream unless you worked in emergency medicine. Even if you did, the people, locations and other details wouldn't be the same. God might convey the same message to you in a similar fashion, but the setting and action will be ones with which you are familiar.

Common tasks can have a spiritual meaning. If you find yourself making copies of a drawing of Jesus at a copy machine, what might that represent? Are believers called to imitate (copy) Him?

Imagine having a dream where you're listening to a message that you don't understand but you're furiously transcribing it, as if you understand it. Is it possible the dream illustrates your need (or ability) to understand the language of heaven? Keep in mind that most dreams illustrate spiritual matters. This will help you understand what elements mean when you see them in a dream. It takes time to develop familiarity with your dream language. But like anything else, if you practice regularly, you'll become more proficient.

As challenging as it can be to interpret your own dreams, interpreting the dreams of others is even more difficult. It requires the interpreter to know the dream environment of a stranger and what the elements of a dream mean to the dreamer. For this reason, I do not routinely provide dream interpretation for others. I prefer teaching them to learn their own dream language so they can interpret their dreams.

CHAPTER TEN

Emotions

WHEN I WITNESS AN EVENT that impacts me personally, my soul creates an emotional response to it. Emotions are reactive. They're created in response to an event and they may lead us to take action. But emotions can mislead us about the severity of potential danger or the blessing hidden in what seems to be an adverse event. Before I take action in response to an event, I set aside my feelings. I try to evaluate the situation as rationally and objectively as I can. I prefer not to rely on my emotions because I know they can mislead me. But when I interpret a dream, I do the exact opposite.

Dreams are dismissed because they're illogical. How many times have you said to yourself a dream didn't make sense? Dreams are not intended to be understood through rational thought. They aren't supposed to make sense. They're received by our spirit and they speak of spiritual realities. One glance at the book of Revelation will tell you that spiritual realities are different from physical ones. Spiritual language is different from natural language. At its core, spiritual language is symbolic and it's *emotional*. It must be interpreted, and many times, the emotion felt in a dream is the interpretive key.

After I've recorded a dream, when I want to interpret it, I ask what emotion was dominant. The emotion we feel while in a dream is the most reliable indicator of how it should be interpreted. Not the emotion we feel *after* the dream, but the one we feel *while* we are dreaming. This is particularly true when the action in a dream would normally evoke one emotion, but the one felt is the opposite. How would you interpret a dream where you watched the destruction of your city while feeling joy or hope? The positive emotion you feel while observing a tragedy is a sign that the dream's meaning is positive. Rather than being about the literal destruction of your city, the dream may speak of the clearing away of old, archaic systems in preparation for something new. Instead of evaluating dreams for their rational content, consider their emotional value and let it guide your interpretation.

Several years ago, I had a dream where I killed an older man who lived down the street from me. In the dream, we were friends and did many things together. I didn't know this man in real life. In the dream, I knew he had to die, so I poisoned him and left him alone at his house. I felt a sadness over killing him, but that emotion quickly turned to a profound sense of peace.

The first clue that this dream was to be interpreted symbolically was that I did not know this man. The second clue was the emotion I felt. If I were to kill someone, I would feel guilt and remorse. I didn't feel the normal emotions because the dream was not intended to be taken literally. As God gave me the interpretation, I understood why I felt peace. In describing our need to walk in a new type of conduct, the Apostle Paul said we should get rid of our "old man" and consider him dead. The "old man" speaks metaphorically, of our former way of living. Killing the "old man" in the dream was symbolic of getting rid of my old ways and submitting myself to God's transformative work. (See Rom 6:6, Eph.4:22, Col.3:9)

Some dreams are devoid of emotion. These dreams are not usually difficult to interpret. In dreams where an emotion is felt, it is given to aid the interpretation and application. Always allow interpretation to be guided by the emotion(s) that are felt during your dream.

CHAPTER ELEVEN

The Meaning of Words and Symbols

To INTERPRET DREAMS, WE MUST determine the meaning of the words, numbers, colors, names and other symbols that appear in them. That task is made more difficult by the fact that meanings of words and symbols are not universal. While the Hebrew meaning of a name will not change over time, the meanings of certain words or symbols may.

Although one can find definitions in a dictionary or online encyclopedia, many words and symbols do not have objective meanings. Meaning is sometimes relative to culture. In western nations, dragons tend to have a negative meaning, but in eastern ones, they carry a positive connotation. Sometimes, the meaning of a word changes rapidly within a particular culture.

The word "bad" has always carried a negative connotation, but in the hippie culture of the 1960s, it suddenly took on a positive meaning.

The word "mother" has always referred to a female parent, but it has other meanings. If you had a dream today where a celebrity said you were a "bad mother," you might be concerned. But if you had the dream in the 1960s, you'd wake with a smile, knowing they may have meant you were a talented musician or actor.

When a word suddenly becomes popular within a cultural group, its meaning changes. In the United States alone, there are thousands of subcultures, each of which assign unique meaning to certain words and symbols. God has given me dreams with symbolic elements that had relevance to a particular culture. When I was familiar with the culture, I understood what the symbols meant. When I was not familiar with the culture, I did not understand their meaning. You might wonder why God would give me dreams containing unfamiliar symbols. It seems He wants me to broaden my horizons and study cultures of which I am not familiar.

In March of 2021, I had a dream where I was shown that writing is one way in which the meanings of words are established. In the absence of writing, words become ambiguous, and symbols have no meaning. As we write, we define what words and symbols mean *to our culture.*

God may give us dreams with words and symbols that have relevance to a culture other than our own. Outside of that culture, it may be difficult to understand them. Unfamiliar cultural references may be most useful when helping someone of another culture interpret their dreams. In these cases, we will need to research the meaning of some words and symbols. That research could include the use of dictionaries and online encyclopedias, but it may also require asking members of the relevant culture what a word or symbol means to them.

CHAPTER TWELVE

Common Dreams

ALTHOUGH EACH DREAM IS UNIQUE, many can be categorized by topic. The subject matter of dreams is surprisingly limited. If you asked millions of people to categorize theirs, you'd find that a handful of dreams have been given to the majority of people. Some spiritual matters are universal; some dreams are ubiquitous. In this chapter, we'll look at a few of the most common dream subjects and their meanings.

Death

A common dream is attending the funeral of a loved one. Less frequently, we may dream of attending our own funeral. These dreams tend to be symbolic rather than literal. They're often accompanied by feelings of joy, hope, or another positive emotion. On rare occasion, God may warn us of the approaching death of a close friend, a relative, or someone we admire. But if the dream comes with a positive emotion, it is usually not about a literal death. More likely, the person in the dream is about to "die" to their old ways and experience a new life, perhaps a new relationship with God. A dream of attending your own funeral may mean you're about to experience the death of an old way of living.

Teeth

Dreams about our teeth are rarely to be interpreted literally. God uses the phrase "wisdom teeth" as a play on words to speak to us about our need for wisdom. At times, we may fall into foolish ways of thinking. A dream about loose, missing, or chipped teeth is generally a wake-up call to change our way of thinking and seek wisdom from God. Problems with an "eye" tooth may suggest an inability to see or discern—spiritually.

Falling

In the literal sense, falling is going from one place or position to another. In the spiritual sense, a similar idea is being illustrated. The Bible warns:

"Pride goes before destruction, And a haughty spirit before a fall"
PROV. 16:18

A dream of falling may warn against becoming prideful. When we fall, we're not in control of our circumstances, at least temporarily. Falling can indicate the approach of an event beyond our control, as when our position in an organization is affected by people above us. If the company you work for as a manager had plans to reduce the number of employees and demote all its managers, you might have a dream of falling. If you held a position in a local church and your position was being eliminated, God might warn you about it in a dream of falling. Note the place from where you fell. It can be a key to the correct interpretation. If a paramedic had a dream of falling off an ambulance, it may portend trouble in the workplace.

Being Naked in Public

It is not unusual to have a dream where you see yourself naked in public. Nakedness represents transparency and openness, while clothing represents concealment and secrecy.

Imagine having a dream where you're in a meeting with your work supervisor. You appear naked, but upon realizing it, you become embarrassed and then try to find clothing to put on. This dream may indicate that you're too transparent and trusting. God may want you to guard yourself more closely. If, on the other hand, you find yourself undressing before your board of directors, it may suggest that you need to be more open and transparent with them.

Past Relationships

When you dream that you're with someone with whom you once had a romantic relationship, it is not normally a sign to reconnect with that person. These dreams are nearly always symbolic. They generally speak of returning to old habits and old ways of thinking. God wants us to move forward into bigger and better things, and these dreams are a warning not to return to the life we once lived. Try researching the meaning of the person's name and you might find another message. For your reference, the last chapter of this book contains the meanings of names.

Bathrooms

The human body is a clever creation. Food and water are put into our bodies, and any products that are not needed are eliminated. Dreams that involve using a toilet, showering, or washing our hands speak of spiritual matters. We all have beliefs, habits, attitudes, biases, and desires that are not beneficial to us. When we hold onto something that God wants us to release for our own good, it may be illustrated in a bathroom dream. The action in the dream may involve a shower, a sink, or a toilet. These dreams are an encouragement to let go of what's holding us back.

Attending School / Taking a Test

Two common dream scenarios are attending school and taking a test. School is where we learn. Attending one in a dream speaks of a need for spiritual instruction. A spiritually immature dreamer may find themselves in elementary school or repeating a class they had already taken. The subject of the class can indicate a spiritual calling. Taking a foreign language class might suggest it's time to learn the spiritual language of speaking in tongues. When we take a test, our knowledge or skill is evaluated. In dreams, it has a similar meaning. God wants us to grow in character. As we do, opportunities are provided to show our progress and reveal areas that still need improvement. When we take an exam in a dream, it's a reminder that a spiritual evaluation is due. The test may involve personal difficulties as this is one way our character is assessed and refined.

Pregnancy

Pregnancy dreams can be frightening. In most cases, they should be interpreted symbolically, and their meaning is almost universal. In a literal pregnancy, a new life is created and nurtured until it can survive on its own. Symbolically, pregnancy speaks of new responsibilities, activities, projects, assignments, ministries, vocations, or hobbies. Anything new to the dreamer's life can be portrayed in a pregnancy dream. Men can have pregnancy dreams too, and the interpretation is the same. If a child is born in a dream and given a name, the meaning of the name may indicate the nature of what God is birthing through you.

Being Chased

In life, when you are being chased, you are in a position of powerlessness. In dreams, the same idea is conveyed, but the application is to spiritual matters. Evil spirits are real entities that oppose us. Dreams of being chased speak of spiritual weakness or immaturity. When we're spiritually immature, we don't know our identity in Christ, and we're subject to being attacked by evil spirits. As we mature, we learn our identity and how to use the weapons of spiritual warfare. Instead of being defenseless targets, we can withstand attacks from the enemy. With practice, evil spirits will one day fear us instead of chasing us. Our spiritual growth may be illustrated in a series of similar dreams.

Hallways and Doors

A hallway is a corridor between two places. It is not a destination in itself. It's the way we reach a destination. In a dream, walking in a hallway suggests that we're on our way to a spiritual destination; a new job, ministry, or calling. A door is a point of entrance. In dreams, they can be an invitation to move into a new thing God has planned.

Losing your Purse, Wallet or Phone

Most of us keep our driver's license or identification card in a purse or wallet. Some keep their identification on their smartphones. When we lose our wallet, purse, or phone in a dream, it's a hint that we've lost our identity in a spiritual sense. We were created as children of God. That is our eternal identity. If we live from some other identity, God may give us one of these dreams to remind us to return to our true identity.

Health

God cares more about our health than we might imagine. If we engage in activities that are dangerous to our health, He may provide a warning. I've been warned on several occasions about the health risks associated with certain behaviors. Although I had been aware of these risks, when God gives you a warning, it's harder to ignore.

Several years ago, I had a dream where I calculated the correct dose of aspirin to take daily. The calculation had to be made according to my body weight. Aspirin is a blood thinner, and some cardiologists recommend it as a preventative against heart attacks. Apparently, God was watching my blood chemistry and wanted me to reduce my risk of having a heart attack. If you receive a dream that seems to speak to a health-related matter, you might consider making whatever lifestyle change is necessary.

Spiders

Spiders commonly appear in dreams. Usually, the dreamer sees them, but not always. Sometimes, they're bitten by one. Spiders and scorpions represent evil spirits. Because they're small, they tend to go unnoticed. Most people don't notice evil spirits, though they can harm both our spiritual and physical health. When spiders or scorpions appear in dreams, it's a warning that an evil spirit is targeting us.

Snakes

Like spiders and scorpions, snakes generally represent the works of darkness. Unlike spiders, snakes are large and conspicuous. While spiders represent evil spirits, snakes symbolize people who oppose us. When the Pharisees opposed Jesus, he called them a brood of vipers.

The type of snake we see in a dream can give us a clue about the specific kind of opposition. Venomous snakes kill their prey by introducing a toxin. Toxins are things like false teaching that can cloud our thinking. A venomous snake might represent someone whose teaching is harmful. (The Pharisees taught that we could please God by keeping the law of Moses.) Anacondas, pythons, and other constrictors kill their prey by squeezing the life out of it. If such a snake appeared in your dream, it might represent someone trying to restrict your activity—perhaps trying to keep you from speaking a truth God has shown you.

Dogs

Dogs are said to be man's best friend. They symbolize companionship or they can represent a threat from the enemy. The action of a dog and the dreamer's emotion will help with the correct interpretation. If you have a dream where a vicious dog is chasing you, it represents the terrorizing work of evil spirits. If you're playing with a dog in a field and feel a positive emotion, it symbolizes friendship. The breed of a dog may illustrate a particular kind of friend. German Shepherds are used for police work and serve as guardians. If you see one in a dream, it may represent someone who acts as a guardian to you. If it is injured, and you feel compassion, it may foretell a coming sickness or injury to them.

Horses

If you consider the word "horsepower," you might guess that in dreams, horses can represent power. If you're riding a horse in a dream, it may illustrate a position of power you currently hold (or one you may hold in the future). Power can be used for both good and evil. The prophet Isaiah warned those who put their trust in the strength (power) of horses and not in God:

> *Woe to those who go down to Egypt for help,*
> *And rely on horses,*
> *Who trust in chariots because they are many,*
> *And in horsemen because they are very strong,*
> *But who do not look to the Holy One of Israel,*
> *Nor seek the Lord!*
> ISA 31:1

Horses may represent concepts other than strength and power. As with every symbol, there can be both positive and negative connotations. Other elements in the dream, the dreamer's emotions, and their attitude toward horses will provide further direction for interpretation.

Flying

Flying dreams illustrate how we operate in the spiritual realm. Flying low to the ground suggests that we have ties to things of the earth. Soaring high in the sky indicates an alignment with God's heavenly plan. If one is unable to control themselves while flying, it represents a lack of self-control in life. Flying at great speed portrays moving in spiritual power.

Storms

Storms are commonly seen in dreams and visions but only rarely are they to be interpreted literally. Storms arrive suddenly and without warning. They cause changes. They're messy, frightening and they interrupt our routines. These things are true about storms in the physical world, and they're true about the changes God brings to our lives. In a word, storms portray *change*. Usually, they hint at sudden, unanticipated changes in life: a change of vocation, a move to a different town, divorce, remarriage, the arrival of a new member to the family, or a sudden change in income. Storm dreams prepare us for coming changes. They can have both positive and negative implications.

Talking on a Phone

Dreams are a form of divine communication. Just as God gives us dreams to convey messages to us, He wants us to communicate with Him. It's common to have a dream where you're talking on your phone with someone, and there are problems with the call. You may hear static and realize you're not being heard. You may have an urgent need to make a call only to realize your phone has no signal. Maybe your phone's battery is dead or has too little power to complete the call. The person you're calling may speak a language you don't understand. What would it mean if, in a dream, someone stole your phone while you were talking to a friend?

All these dreams symbolize communication problems. Something is preventing you from communicating with someone you cannot see. In most dreams, we speak face to face with people we can see. But often, people we cannot literally see are portrayed as someone we talk with on the phone. Sometimes, the unseen person is a symbolic stand-in for God. Interruptions in a phone conversation may suggest that the cares of life are interfering in our relationship with God. A dead battery or no signal implies that we've stopped communicating with God. When something interferes with this relationship, the problem is always on our end. God is never too busy to talk to us. He's always available and willing to discuss the issues of life. These dreams are a gentle invitation to start a new conversation.

Rapture Dreams

In January of 2012, I had a dream where I watched three people who loved God being taken into heaven. No one else went to heaven except them. There was no suggestion that Jesus was about to return to earth. I wasn't certain, but the last person I saw taken into heaven may have been me. This person wrote a note telling his friends he had not been abducted, but that God had taken him into heaven. How we interpret these dreams depends on our view of God and the future.

Many people believe we're living in the last days before the return of Jesus. In some views of the future, Christians are removed from the earth and taken bodily into heaven before His return. If a dreamer holds this view of the future, they may interpret these dreams as a sign of the impending return of Jesus. But there is another interpretation.

The fourth chapter of the book of Revelation opens with the Apostle John being taken into heaven to see the things God wanted to show Him. This scene is the Biblical model of this kind of dream. John was told by God to "come up here," and somehow, he was able to (at least temporarily) visit heaven. It is not widely taught, but there is an implication here that God wants us to draw near to Him, even on occasion, visiting Him in heaven.

John's gospel records a discussion between Jesus and Thomas.

> *"Let not your heart be troubled; you believe in God, believe also in Me. In My Father's house are many mansions; if it were not so, I would have told you. I go to prepare a place for you. And if I go and prepare a place for you, I will come again and receive you to Myself; that where I am, there you may be also. And where I go you know, and the way you know."*
>
> *Thomas said to Him, "Lord, we do not know where You are going, and how can we know the way?"*
>
> *Jesus said to him, "I am the way, the truth, and the life. No one comes to the Father except through Me.*
> JOHN 14:1-6

Many people think that all we need is a relationship with Jesus. But in this conversation, the Son of God explained that He wants to lead us into a relationship with His Father. He went to prepare a place for us, that where He is, we may be also. He is in heaven, and He wants us to join Him there. Must we physically die before we visit heaven? The Apostle John's experience suggests it isn't necessary. God has shown me important tasks that can be carried out in the heavenly realms, including the courts of heaven, which I describe in my book *Defeating Your Adversary in the Courts of Heaven*. Dreams of being taken into heaven may encourage us to explore these possibilities.

CHAPTER THIRTEEN

Common Dream Elements

ALMOST ANY PERSON, PLACE, OR thing can symbolize a concept in a dream. A few symbolic elements appear more commonly than others. Commonly appearing elements tend to have a more consistent meaning. Buildings, vehicles, people, colors, and numbers are a few of the elements that reliably convey messages in dreams. In this chapter, we'll identify common dream elements and discuss their meaning.

Vehicles

A vehicle is a mode of transportation. A boat, car, airplane, train, bus, or helicopter gets you from one place to another. The size, age, and speed of the vehicle you use in life is determined by your needs. You wouldn't take a passenger airplane to the grocery store, and you wouldn't use a convertible to transport a church congregation. Each kind of vehicle is designed for a specific use. When vehicles appear in dreams they speak to specific issues in our lives.

In dreams, vehicles represent the way we operate in the spiritual realm. The vehicle, especially if we are operating it, is a representation of us. Its size, speed, color, age, and how it operates illustrate functions of our spiritual life. Sometimes, a vehicle represents aspects of our ministry to others.

Any vehicle powered by your own strength, like a bicycle or canoe, may symbolize working in our own power as opposed to the power of God's Spirit. Vehicles with powerful engines symbolize great spiritual power.

Sometimes a vehicle is a particular color because it represents the actual vehicle we own (or did own at one time). In these cases, no significance is attached to the color of the vehicle. In other cases, where the vehicle is not one you own, the color may represent some aspect of your life. (See the symbols dictionary for the meaning of specific colors.)

What if you're driving a car down a steep grade in a dream without the ability to stop? An out-of-control car represents an out-of-control life. A dream that you're driving a car that continually swerves into oncoming traffic also represents a lack of self-control. These dreams are warnings to exercise restraint and self-control. Self-control is a fruit of our relationship with God (see Gal 5:22).

Let's consider the following dream: The dreamer is driving the car they currently own. One front tire is flat, but they keep going. It's difficult to see; it's night and the car's headlights are dim. Although the dreamer has no plan to turn left or right, the turn signal is on, and the dreamer is unable to turn it off. A police car pulls them over as the dream ends. Now, let's interpret the dream.

A car's tires allow it to move smoothly. A flat tire hinders progress; therefore, something is preventing the dreamer from reaching their spiritual destination. Headlights enable us to see what is in front of us. Dim headlights can represent poor spiritual foresight. The dreamer may be blindsided by some event they should have seen coming. Turn signals indicate a change of direction. The car's turn signal was on, but the dreamer was not changing direction, and they were unable to cancel the turn indicator. This suggests that the dreamer may be reluctant to accept needed changes or realize changes are needed. Police represent spiritual authority or leadership. Being pulled over by police in a dream usually symbolizes a need for correction from someone who can provide wise counsel.

You may have a dream where you're driving a car while looking into the rear-view mirror. A rear-view mirror shows what is behind us. Gazing at one symbolizes looking into our past. While there's nothing wrong with reflecting on our past, if we obsess over mistakes, especially if we condemn ourselves, it can be unhealthy. Emotional healing can help in dealing with unresolved issues from our past; this could be the message of such a dream.

A friend had a dream years ago where he was piloting a large passenger ship. Passenger vehicles often represent church congregations. My friend is a mature prophetic leader. God was showing him that he would soon lead a larger group.

About ten years ago, I had a dream where I was co-piloting a spaceship. I worked beside a more experienced pilot. We went on several missions, including one where we encountered another space ship piloted by someone who wasn't qualified to fly solo. We did what we could to get them to land safely, though the other pilot caused problems by being careless in how he flew. When we landed, my pilot reported him to the authorities. Spaceships operate in deep space. Flying one in a dream suggests a ministry that operates in the deeper mysteries of God. My position as co-pilot indicated I was in spiritual training when I had the dream. In this kind of ministry, dangers exist, and operating safely is of prime importance.

When we operate a vehicle in a dream, it tends to portray aspects of our personal ministry to others, even if that ministry is to a handful of people. The age of a vehicle may illustrate a period of time when certain types of ministries were popular. At various times during the last two centuries, healing and revival ministries were prominent. Driving a car built during that era may suggest a ministry that was popular at the time. I once had a dream where I was building a car from the chassis of two different models. The front half was a model from the 1930s. The back half was a model from the 1940s. The dream spoke of needing to connect two cultural movements that were popular at different time periods.

In 2013, I had a dream with two scenes. In the first part of the dream, I spoke with someone as we looked at the engine of a car. (I did not know the person I spoke with.) I viewed the engine from above and below. The engine was unusual in that it had flexible metal intake and exhaust manifolds. (Most cars have manifolds made of cast iron or aluminum). I noted that the engine had an in-line eight-cylinder configuration and later learned it was a rare and powerful model. In the second scene of the dream, I watched a man carefully work his way through the steps necessary to make a strategic move that would bring financial prosperity, which he would use to further God's kingdom.

Engines speak of power. Spiritual power is used for healing and miracles. It seems that God had planned to give someone a unique healing ministry through which they could fund advancement of His kingdom.

I one had a related dream where I rebuilt an engine. As I assembled the parts, I thought of how I might decrease wear on the parts so they wouldn't need to be repaired as often. I was inspired to use a different type of oil that wouldn't break down. It would protect the parts from friction and wear and the engine would last longer. The Holy Spirit is frequently represented by oil. As we interact with others, we create friction, which can lead to interpersonal problems. The grace of God motivates us to forgive others. Like oil, it prevents friction and keeps our relationships intact.

Your House

Just as vehicles represent features of our lives, houses represent aspects of our life that God wants to address. When a specific room in a house is the scene of a dream, it can illustrate matters that pertain to a particular part of life. As noted previously, bathrooms, when they are the focal point of a dream, reveal parts of our life that need cleansing. Bedrooms are where we rest. A bedroom dream may speak of a need for spiritual rest, but more often, bedrooms are the backdrop of dreams where God addresses matters of intimacy with Him. The Bible book Song of Songs is a romantic and highly figurative portrayal of man's relationship with God.

Let him kiss me with the kisses of his mouth—
For your love is better than wine.
Because of the fragrance of your good ointments,
Your name is ointment poured forth;
Therefore the virgins love you.
Draw me away!
We will run after you.
The king has brought me into his chambers.
We will be glad and rejoice in you.
We will remember your love more than wine.
Rightly do they love you.
SONG 1:1-4

If a person appears in a bedroom dream and makes romantic overtures toward you, they might be a stand-in for God. If your relationship with Him is distant, expect Him to draw you closer through these dreams. When we draw close to God, He discusses personal matters, like our honesty, integrity, faithfulness, charity, obedience, compassion, or perseverance. I've found that when He corrects me in some area, He does it in the kindest way, and He's quick to praise me when I make needed changes.

Anything God uses can become a tool of an enemy. Bedroom dreams with explicit sex scenes can come from evil spirits and draw us into sexual immorality. Dreams with dark colors, dim lighting, and negative emotions are signs of the enemy's handiwork. If you resist sexual immorality, evil spirits will find someone else to harass, and these dreams will be less common.

When we aren't using our car, we keep it in a garage. If you have a dream where you're sitting in the car you currently own, but the car is idling in your garage, it may suggest that you've been less active than you should be. The dream might be an encouragement to get back in the game. Conversely, after a long stretch of activity, you might have a dream where you're driving for a long time. At the end of the dream, you pull your car into your garage. This dream might hint that rest is needed.

We prepare food in a kitchen. Food represents spiritual nutrition. I've had dreams where I was in my kitchen preparing food for guests. A major focus of my ministry is teaching. Before I can share a lesson with others, I have to prepare it. My kitchen dreams speak of preparing teaching material for others.

A dining room is similar to a kitchen, but it's where food is served. Symbolically, it's where we gather with others for spiritual growth and fellowship. Jesus' last supper with His disciples is the archetype of the dining room dream.

We gather with friends and relatives in a living room, and this is where God illustrates our spiritual relationships with others. I've had dreams where friends visited me in my living room, and a worship service broke out. In others, I've seen myself praying with a group of friends or giving them prophetic words in my living room.

On the day of Pentecost, God visited the disciples in the upper room, and they received the baptism of the Holy Spirit. While the first floor of a house is nearest to the earth, the second floor is closest to heaven. In the upper floor(s) of a house, the mysteries of God's kingdom are revealed. A friend once had a dream where I visited their home. I went up a flight of stairs and opened the door to a second floor they were unaware of. This dream revealed that there are things about God which they did not know.

An attic is the highest room in a house, and it may be the scene where deep mysteries are revealed. It's also where we store things over long periods. Memories are stored in our soul. Issues from our past may be illustrated in dreams that take place in an attic. Those who suffer emotional trauma may dream about the attic of their childhood home.

The basement of a house is not visible to the public. It's generally dark and can be a habitat for spiders. Symbolically, basements represent dark areas of our lives that we have not allowed God to address.

Secret sins and false beliefs that we hold privately can be portrayed in basement dreams.

The front porch, front yard, and windows that view them speak of things in front of us. Symbolically, they portray present or future events or issues that are known to the public. The back yard, back porch, and windows that view them symbolize our past or issues that are private.

I had a dream a few years ago where a friend gathered dead sticks and piles of trash from his back yard and threw them in a bonfire he had made at the edge of his property. The dream was during a season where many friends went through emotional healing. It symbolized my friend's decision to let God heal him of the wounds he had received years ago.

The condition or appearance of a house can reveal an issue God wants to address. A friend told me of a dream in which he was shown a glass house that was beautifully decorated. My friend is a piano player and often has dreams featuring a piano. In this dream one was prominently displayed near the entry of the house. The glass house represented transparency. God was calling him to live in such a way that he didn't feel the need to hide anything.

My wife once had a dream that it was snowing inside the house where we currently lived. Snow and things that are white in color often represent purity and newness.

Buildings

Buildings that appear in dreams usually represent institutions of society such as government agencies, the media, the church, the medical industry, the entertainment industry or academia. Frequently, the type of building and what happens in it can convey a message from God.

Over a span of several years, my wife had dreams where the setting was always a hotel. Each dream featured a different building. Hotels speak of transition—or going from one place to another. During this season, God brought many new things into our lives; we were in a constant state of change.

I became a Christian in the year 2000. For seven years, I attended a church that taught the Bible, but did not teach healing, dreams or anything supernatural. I began having dreams and visions in 2008. Many of them illustrated aspects of church life that God wanted me to understand.

I had a dream in 2010 about a reunion with people I once knew. We came together to play volleyball. At the beginning of the dream, I entered a building through a long, white tent that resembled the tabernacle in the wilderness as it was described in the Old Testament. Food was abundant inside. I went in and took an elevator to the second floor. After leaving the elevator, I found myself in a volleyball game. When it was my turn to serve the ball, I never lost the side. Nobody could return my serves. Some dropped just over the net; some curved as they approached people so that they couldn't hit it back. Near the end, I served a loaf of bread wrapped in aluminum foil to a woman. It curved away from her as she tried to hit it. After picking it up, she walked over and asked how I made the ball do that. I then used the elevator to return to the first floor. I left the building through the white tabernacle and saw older adults eating food. They seemed feeble and moved very slowly. They only ate one type of food and never ate anything different, though there was a wide variety of food available. At this point, the dream shifted to a beach.

In the final scene, I was on a beach with younger people, near a structure resembling a lifeguard stand that stood at the edge of the water. Although this was a sandy beach, there was deep water directly in front of the lifeguard stand. It seemed obvious to me, but no one else saw it. I talked with the people who were there and tried to convince them it was safe to jump in the water in front of the lifeguard stand. They weren't convinced it was safe, so I climbed up on the stand, jumped in, and did not touch the bottom. Someone followed my lead, and before long, others were jumping in, too.

Now, let's interpret the dream. I rarely have dreams where the setting is a building. But I had been trying to interact with local church congregations at that time and faced many obstacles. The dream pointed out some of them. The tabernacle represents the institutional church. It's white. It looks nice, and there's plenty of food (teaching), though few

Christians want variety. Most are happy to eat the same food (learn the same lessons repeatedly). I quickly left that setting, meaning I would not remain connected to these church congregations. God had other plans.

The second floor represented a closer relationship with God. But the volleyball game revealed a similar problem. Even when I engaged in a higher level of spiritual activity (healing, miracles, deliverance), people could not receive what I served them (they could not receive my teaching). The beach scene showed where I was supposed to be. Outside the church walls, showing a small group of people the deeper mysteries of God's kingdom, discussing their fears, and leading by example.

Around that time, I had other, similar dreams with similar messages. One night, I had two of these dreams. In the first dream, I was in a warehouse. I saw a brief flash of the warehouse full of exotic sports cars, packed wall to wall. Then the warehouse went dark, and was empty. Next, I heard a door open, the rev of an engine, and saw a sports car drive in.

Immediately after this dream, I had a second one where I was in a tall building. The roof was about 200 feet from the floor. The building was dark; I could only make out a few objects. I tried to position a ladder so I could climb to a loft. No matter where I placed it, the ladder swayed too much to be climbed safely. I moved it to one spot, and it nearly fell over. Then, I was given a view of a dusty loft. Piles of junk were stacked from floor to ceiling. I knew I needed to get something from the loft, but I didn't know what it was or where it was located. I never climbed the ladder. I knew it was pointless to go up there because I had been up there before. The last time I had this dream, I was in the loft looking for something. I hated being there. It was dusty, dark, drafty, and disgusting. I moved things around for what seemed like an eternity but never found what I was looking for. In the dream, it wasn't clear what I was searching for, but it seemed I was looking in the wrong place. This was the content of the second dream.

In the dreams of Christians, buildings often represent the institutional church. That was true here. One building had many bright, new, powerful cars (representing powerful ministries); the other was a dead, dark, dusty place with relics for which I had no use. The dark building represented the frustrating situation I faced at the time. I tried to influence local churches, but no one was interested. God had previously told me that what I wanted couldn't be found inside the institutional church. The sports cars (powerful ministries) would be the manifestation of a new thing. The glimpse of sports cars in the warehouse was a preview of coming attractions. The new model of the church would be built one person at a time. The first car driving into the warehouse represented the beginning of this new movement. Cars are stored in a warehouse until they're used. This suggests that these people would first be gathered and then put to work.

Colors

Colors are important symbolic elements in dreams, particularly when a vehicle, house, or item of clothing is a certain color. The color black usually (though not always) represents things of darkness. Black cats and birds may symbolize evil spirits. However, God sent ravens to feed the prophet Elijah in the wilderness. Black birds do not always symbolize evil. We must consider the context of the dream and the dreamer's emotions.

In the Bible, heavenly beings are often described as having white hair and wearing white garments. White tends to symbolize the things of heaven, purity and cleanness. As always, the context of the dream must be considered before assigning meaning. If you have a dream where a man driving a white van is robbing people in your neighborhood, the odds are that the color white in this context does not mean he's an agent of God. If, on the other hand, he's delivering food, the color white may symbolize a divine mission.

Red is a highly symbolic color. It usually speaks of the blood of Jesus, which was shed for our redemption. Red symbolizes love and passion but may also speak of hatred and anger. Green typically represents life, but it can also represent envy. Blue often represents the Holy Spirit and spiritual life, but depression and sadness are called "the blues." Other colors may appear in dreams. Their symbolic meaning can be found in the Bible or the symbol dictionary at the back of this book.

Numbers

You may find certain numbers mentioned or highlighted in your dreams. Although a number may have its literal meaning, it may convey a symbolic message. If you had a dream where a stranger said, "The answer is seven." You might look up the number seven in the Bible. The number seven is mentioned hundreds of times and generally refers to divine completion or fullness. God completed the creation in seven days. In the book of Revelation, we find the letters Jesus sent to seven churches in Asia. These churches represent all churches throughout history. In a dream where a stranger says, "The answer is seven," God may be saying He and His kingdom are the sum of everything that has meaning.

The number twelve frequently appears in dreams. Like seven, it appears hundreds of times in the Bible. The nation of Israel had twelve tribes, there were twelve stones in the breastplate of the high priest, and Jesus chose twelve men to be His disciples. Twelve often represents God's governmental rule.

Ten is another symbolic number. When the prophet Daniel and his friends were taken captive in Babylon, they refused to drink the wine and eat the King's delicacies that were set before them. They asked their masters to test them for ten days and permit them to eat only vegetables and drink only water.

In the book of Revelation, we find this verse:

> Do not fear any of those things which you are about to suffer. Indeed, the devil is about to throw some of you into prison, that you may be tested, and you will have tribulation ten days. Be faithful until death, and I will give you the crown of life.
> REV. 2:10

These passages and others suggest that ten represents testing.

The number four may be highlighted in a dream. There are four cardinal points on a compass—north, south, east, and west. Numbers often appear in the book of Revelation, including the number four.

> *After these things I saw four angels standing at the four corners of the earth, holding the four winds of the earth, that the wind should not blow on the earth, on the sea, or on any tree.*
> REV. 7:1

The number four often represents matters that have a global impact. These are just a few of the numbers you might find in dreams. Other numbers are included in the section on dream symbols. Keep in mind that every number has several possible meanings, and sometimes, they can be understood literally.

Names

In ancient Hebrew culture, every name had a meaning. When Abraham and Isaac named their children, they prophesied each one's destiny. Just as names had meaning back then, when a name is known in a dream, it often conveys a message. Sometimes a name will be spoken. Other times, a person will appear, and you will know their name. In either case, note the name and look up its meaning. This includes the names of people, cities, streets, boats, and anything else with a prominent name.

You might have a dream where a friend named David appears. Nothing much happens in it. Your friend sits beside you. He smiles, and the dream ends. You might dismiss this as a pointless soul dream, but what would you think if I said the Hebrew meaning of the name David is "beloved?" If the dream happened on February 14th, could it be that God sent you a valentine's dream? Don't dismiss a dream because it seems too simple to be profound. Sometimes merely interpreting a name will unlock the meaning of a dream. The last chapter of this book contains hundreds of names along with their meaning. If you need to know the meaning of a name not included in the chapter, most baby name websites that can provide that information.

Weapons

Every day you spend on planet earth is a day in which you will battle spirits that are bent on destroying you. If it does not *seem* like such a battle is occurring, you are not fully aware of the spiritual realm. Paul described this spiritual battle and some of our spiritual weapons in the sixth chapter of his letter to the church in Ephesus:

> *Finally, my brethren, be strong in the Lord and in the power of His might. Put on the whole armor of God, that you may be able to stand against the wiles of the devil. For we do not wrestle against flesh and blood, but against principalities, against powers, against the rulers of the darkness of this age, against spiritual hosts of wickedness in the heavenly places. Therefore, take up the whole armor of God, that you may be able to withstand in the evil day, and having done all, to stand.*
>
> *Stand therefore, having girded your waist with truth, having put on the breastplate of righteousness, and having shod your feet with the preparation of the gospel of peace; above all, taking the shield of faith with which you will be able to quench all the fiery darts of the wicked one. And take the helmet of salvation, and the sword of the Spirit, which is the word of God; praying always with all prayer and supplication in the Spirit, being watchful to this end with all perseverance and supplication for all the saints— and for me, that utterance may be given to me, that I may open my mouth boldly to make known the mystery of the gospel, for which I am an ambassador in chains; that in it I may speak boldly, as I ought to speak.*
> EPH 6:10-19

Anyone who sincerely tries to draw close to God will face opposition from evil spirits. If you desire to learn about healing or deliverance, you can expect them to oppose you every step of the way. God has provided spiritual weapons and tactics that allow us to defeat them.

My introduction to spiritual weaponry was illustrated in a dream in 2008. In it, I drove my car to a pawn shop with my two children and traded some things I owned for a strange type of gun. My kids waited a long time for me to come out. I left the shop with my new gun but didn't want the kids to see it, so I walked to a spot behind my car then took it out and examined it. The gun had a laser sight and was wide, with a round bulge that seemed to be where ammunition was stored.

It wasn't a revolver, and it didn't have a magazine. I didn't know how the ammunition was loaded. I tried to figure out how it worked and aimed it across the street at a vacant lot. The gun fired two rounds, which I wouldn't have known, except that I saw puffs of dust rise from the ground where I pointed it. The weapon made no sound and didn't have a trigger, but fired by my thoughts. I put it in the trunk of my car, and that was the end of the dream. Now, let's interpret it.

I traded things I had obtained from the world for a new weapon. This speaks of changing paradigms and acquiring a new way of thinking. I had to leave behind the mode of thinking I had used in the world and learn the one used in God's kingdom. I took my kids with me when I acquired the gun. This implies that although the issue of weaponry applied to me, at some point, I would need to teach it to my children. I was unskilled at the time, so I kept the weapon hidden until I learned how to use it. I was in the pawnshop for a long time before coming out. This suggests that acquiring spiritual weaponry is not a quick process. It takes time, and those who are watching might have to wait for us. The gun was activated by my thoughts or as I exercised my will. Spiritual warfare is often a matter of how we choose to exert our will. Ultimately, God and Satan both want us to surrender our will to them. The one to whom we submit our will is the one we serve. Part of our spiritual training is learning to submit our will to God.

Let's look at another dream. In this one, I was on a trip with friends as we visited a demon infested island. We stayed on one end of the island and remained tightly grouped together for safety. A few people left the group and were harassed by demons. Those who dared to wander farthest from the group got the worst of it. I was given a close-up view of the other end of the island. I came to know that there were one million demons on the island and that the people who lived there permanently were severely demonized—to the point of insanity.

The interpretation isn't difficult. One purpose of the dream was to make me aware that demons are real. It also revealed that they could make people mentally ill. Further, it illustrated that the key to safety is being surrounded and protected by other believers, and the surest way to become a casualty is to wander away from them. Lastly, it suggests that the number of demons we're fighting is almost innumerable.

Now, let's look at a frightening dream I had. In this dream, I was with a group of people who planned to pull off a bank robbery. If you've seen the film *Reservoir Dogs,* you have an idea of what happened in the dream. We'd planned the perfect heist. We would enter the bank, ask for the money and leave without anyone getting hurt. But in the dream, as soon as we entered the bank, all hell broke loose. The authorities immediately knew a robbery was in progress. Gunfire erupted. People screamed as they were caught in a hail of bullets.

Suddenly, I found myself on the top floor of the building, where I saw dead and wounded people lying all around me on the floor. There were five or six men with guns trying to kill me. I sensed this was a battle to the death. I knew with certainty that if I didn't kill them, they would kill me. So, with a cool head and extreme determination, I dodged their gunfire and systematically hunted and executed every one of them—even those who were wounded. After killing the last enemy, I went into the elevator, where I found a paramedic kit and uniform. I put on the uniform, and as the door opened on the ground floor, I found an EMT partner and a gurney. We grabbed an injured person, put them on the gurney, and made our way to the front door. I got out of the building without anyone questioning me.

You might wonder why God would give me such a violent dream. I think one reason is that He knew it would be memorable. The dream was so shocking that years later, I still remember the details. Second-ly, the dream wasn't merely violent; it closely resembled the plot of *Reservoir Dogs,* a film that had deeply impacted me. God knew I would appreciate the gravity of the situation he was illustrating because of how that film had affected me.

Five years ago, I had no idea the measures that would be taken to silence me. In 2020, I was banned from all major social media plat-forms. I'm slandered by the mainstream media. My payment gateways have been closed and my most popular books have been blacklisted. I underestimated the resistance I would face. I thought my enemy had been neutralized. God wanted me to know I'm engaged in a vicious fight against a well-armed and determined opponent. Victory will take every ounce of commitment and determination I can muster. My survival depends on skillfully using the weapons of spiritual warfare.

Military Dreams

Just as dreams of weapons can symbolize spiritual warfare, dreams of being in the military can portray life as a spiritual soldier. In 2009, I had a dream where I was hiding from an enemy that wanted me dead. In the opening scene, I walked along a road. Then, I entered a wooded area and met up with soldiers in BDUs (battle dress uniforms). I became a soldier, and my clothing turned into a uniform. We made our way through the woods without being detected, then came to a house and went into the basement.

Through a window, we watched other soldiers perform a musical number from a hit Broadway play called *M-1*. They executed perfect formations while singing songs and occasionally, firing their rifles. Then, the building changed to a house.

I stayed in that house for a couple of days with a woman I didn't know. I slept in a screened porch on an army cot. The woman slept beside me on her own cot. (In dreams, a woman sometimes symbolizes the church, i.e., other believers). At one point in the dream, a phone rang, and I answered it. The caller pretended to be a friend, but I knew they were my enemy. I looked out the window and saw a sniper on a hillside about a half-mile away, ready to shoot me. The sniper was the person on the phone. They were trying to verify my location, but I told them I was somewhere else. The woman next to me didn't know what was going on. I knew I was about to be shot, so I yelled out, "SNIPER!" I quickly rolled off the cot onto the floor as a bullet came through the screen but missed me. I picked up the phone and taunted the caller telling him he was a crappy sniper. Suddenly, a shower of bullets ripped through the wall as we were under heavy gunfire. I taunted the shooter again, "You must be the worst sniper in the world if you can't even kill me with an automatic rifle."

At this point, I left the house, realizing I needed a safer place to stay. I went to a large hospital, put on scrubs, and blended in with the staff. I pretended to be a hospital employee for a couple of days and slept on the top floor in a doctor's suite. Some days, I would pretend to work in housekeeping; other days, I acted like a technician. I wore a surgical mask to hide my face and avoided anyone who may have been looking for me. As long as I was in the hospital, I felt safe. Let's interpret this dream.

The soldiers I met while walking on the road were other believers. The performance we watched displayed the power of worship as a form of warfare. Worship is a more powerful weapon than I had realized. The sniper who tried to kill me represented an evil spirit. In reality, even when I'm confronted with death, I remain optimistic and sarcastic. My activities in the hospital represented my ministry in the field of health care. I never experienced a direct threat in that setting. The key to my success when I worked as a paramedic was looking like everyone else, functioning in the gifts God has given me, and not drawing attention to myself.

The Unknown Person

I've had many dreams where I watched an unknown person doing something. In one dream, I watched them make changes to a website. In another, they wrote a book on a certain subject. In a third, they addressed an audience about a particular matter. It took a while to understand who this person was. I thought perhaps it was me, but sometimes, the action they took was not one I would take. That fact led me to consider the possibility that the unknown person was God, whose actions and thoughts are not like ours.

> *"For My thoughts are not your thoughts, Nor are your ways My ways," says the Lord.*
> ISA 55:8

Once you accept that your life needs fine-tuning, you may see an improved version of yourself in the anonymous person of your dreams. In these dreams, the unknown person typically leads by example. We observe them doing things we need to do.

Sometimes, a faceless, silent person who appears in a dream will be the driver of our car, or the kind soul who helps us in battle. When you are both in the same dream, the anonymous person is usually the Spirit of God.

The Other You

Just as a better version of you may be portrayed as an anonymous person, a wounded version of you may show up in a dream. I found an alternate version of myself during a season of emotional healing.

A few years ago, a friend named Matt spent several hours helping me receive healing of childhood trauma. After the first session, we knew more healing was needed. My goal for the second session was to find the "other me."

Matt started the second session like he usually does, asking the Holy Spirit to reveal different things about me. God revealed secrets to him only a few people knew, like the fact that despite being an extrovert, I often prefer long periods of seclusion. Everything revealed to him hinted at the existence of another me—a persona that was unknown to me, except through occasional mood swings, and a dream, which I will share next.

In the dream, I saw two versions of myself. One "me" was outgoing and loved to socialize. The other "me" lived in a cave and wanted to be left alone. In the dream, the outgoing me counseled the cave-dwelling me and tried to convince him it was safe to come out of the cave.

Most people suffer emotional trauma, which creates a fragmented soul. These fragments are called alters (short for alternate personalities). I'd never thought about whether I had an alter or how one might affect my behavior. But the dream made me aware that I had at least one, and eventually, I would have to deal with it.

As Matt continued, I told him what I saw in my mind. Before long, we found the alter, living in a cavern, somewhere inside of me. The usual method of healing an alter is to have them meet with Jesus. So, Matt asked Jesus to find my alter. In my mind, I saw Jesus standing in the cave beside my alter.

The alter had one concern. I've expressed it at various times through-out my life, mostly when I'm under pressure to conform to people's expectations. The concern was that no one understands me. So, the alter asked Jesus if He understood him. Jesus said He did. Then he asked if he could be trusted. Jesus answered that He could be trusted. When the alter was satisfied with the answers, he went with Jesus. They came out of the cave together and immediately went into heaven.

We found two more alters who were toddlers, sitting with Jesus in the living room of the house I lived in 50 years ago. We said healing prayers for them, and they went with Jesus. When the healing session was over, I felt physically tired. But emotionally, I felt great.

Emotional trauma happens to everyone. It fragments our soul, and these fragments may show up in dreams as a different version of us. If you suffered trauma in childhood, you might see yourself as a wounded or confused child. Jesus can heal the alters and help you live a more balanced, normal life. If you'd like to explore this subject further, I wrote a fictional allegory about emotional healing called *The Gates of Shiloh.*

CHAPTER FOURTEEN

Common Dream Themes

WE'VE LOOKED AT THE MOST common dreams people have. Then, we examined common elements that appear in dreams and what they represent. Now, we'll look at common dream themes. A *theme* is an overarching principle. If you had to summarize the message of a dream in one word, you might state its theme. If, for example, you had a dream where soldiers stood guard outside your home, you might say the theme was *protection.*

The theme may also be the purpose for which a dream is given. If, for example, you have a dream where a friend was putting curses on you, and you later find out they practice witchcraft, you might say God gave you the dream as a *warning.*

God has many purposes for giving us dreams. The following list is not exhaustive, but it does provide an overview of the most common themes.

Warning

Depending on your lifestyle, many of the dreams you receive may warn of impending danger. When I worked as a paramedic, I regularly had dreams about EMT partners. In one dream, I was looking for a new partner as I drove my car through an urban setting. A man approached and asked if I was looking for a new partner. He tried to get in my car, but I sensed he was evil, so I swerved away quickly and drove off before he could get in. This dream was not about a new EMT partner. It was a warning that an evil spirit was trying to come into my life (symbolized by my car) to gain influence over me.

Years ago, I had a dream that a friend was in a car accident. He wasn't injured, but his vehicle wasn't drivable so he called to ask if I could give him a ride home, which I did. Seven months later, the same friend was a passenger in a head-on collision that took the life of the driver. My friend sustained rib fractures which healed quickly. I didn't know it at the time, but he had been having an affair with the woman who was killed. The incident destroyed him, emotionally. After a long time of self-examination, He turned his life over to God and now leads a changed life. The dream informed me that at some point, my friend's life would be ruined (in the dream, his car was not drivable) and that I would need to help him (I gave him a ride home).

In recent years, I've received many dreams about problems with my website. Some of the dreams have revealed new malware infections. Others showed how my website was about to come under coordinated attack. One dream revealed problems with my website's ability to send and receive emails from visitors. Over the years, God has always warned me whenever a new problem with my website was about to show up. In some cases, a dream revealed not just the nature of the problem, but the solution.

When I was new to spiritual warfare, I was often warned about attacks by evil spirits and people who opposed me. Some of these warning dreams pertained to health issues. Some were about my personal safety. Others were about financial or occupational changes. All warning dreams are intended to prepare us for situations about which we may not be aware.

Encouragement

Dreams of encouragement are intended to help us persevere in difficult times. The nature of the dream will depend on the subject for which the dreamer needs encouragement.

Over the years, as my website has grown in popularity, I've received more negative comments on my articles. A year before the negative comments showed up, I had several dreams where I was learning to deal with them. In the dreams, I saw more and more mean and hateful comments appear on my posts. In the way that you know something in a dream, I knew I needed to ignore these comments instead of responding to them. Those who made the negative comments were trying to discourage me. For the sake of those who appreciated my messages, I knew I needed to keep writing. Predictably, a year later, when my website received more traffic, more hateful and discouraging comments showed up. As in the dreams, I ignored them and focused on the feedback from people who enjoyed my articles and videos.

Direction

One day, after watching three videos on spiritual travel featuring Bruce Allen, I had a dream where I was discussing the subject with a group of people. I was clarifying my position and writing about the subject. This was one of the first dreams confirming that I should explore traveling in the spirit.

I once had a dream where I was taking a freshman English class. It seemed as though I should have taken the class years earlier as I was much older than the other students. I had fun making jokes with the teacher, but I could see she had back pain from the way she walked. I felt as though I should have prayed for her to be healed, but I didn't pray for her. I left the classroom and wandered around the school building not knowing where I was going next. Let's interpret this dream.

Although I had developed competency in healing, the dream indicated I had been delinquent in mastering the English language. It was given after I had published my first book. If I intended to write professionally, I would need to become more knowledgeable in the use of punctuation, grammar, spelling and sentence structure. In addition, I didn't show the concern I might have about the teacher's back pain, which suggests a lack of compassion. I left the classroom and wandered aimlessly around the school building, which suggests a lack focus and commitment to learning.

One night I had a dream where I spoke with a friend about how to make a boring Facebook conversation livelier. We went all the way back to the beginning of our friendship and found our first conversation thread. I showed her how to ask various questions about a subject to make the conversation more interesting. This dream illustrated that if we are intentional, we can facilitate meaningful discussions online.

Several years ago, I made a trip to Sedona, Arizona—a place famous for its New Age culture. The night I returned home, I had a dream where I taught New Age practitioners about various aspects of God's kingdom, including healing. In the last scene of the dream, I prayed for people to be healed, and said that if any of them were not healed, I would enroll them in my healing class for free. I had not developed a healing class at this time, but the dream caused me to create a video-based healing class, which is available on my website. The following night, I had a long, detailed dream about healing survivors of Satanic ritual abuse.

I once had a dream where several people misunderstood the things I said about God, mainly having to do with His sovereignty. I corrected their misunderstandings. It's easy to misunderstand someone's message. I've often been misunderstood, but over the years, I've made an effort to be as clear and unambiguous as possible about my views.

Years ago, I had a dream where I was reminding believers to gather together on Sundays. In the dream, I knew they had not been coming together, so I gave a series of messages (each message was the same) encouraging them to gather for fellowship. The point was not to hear a message, but to come together and discuss the issues of life. I knew I had delivered the messages online, though strangely, I was speaking to each audience in person. This dream was one of the first that suggested I should consider hosting live broadcasts to build a community. If you ask God for direction, He will provide it—often in great detail.

Instruction

God may teach us virtually anything in a dream. I once had a dream where I was given a bag of Facebook "likes." I knew I had to use them all because the next day I would receive another bag of them. At the time I had this dream, I was active on Facebook and many of my dreams highlighted how I should conduct myself. This dream reminded me to encourage others as often as possible (by liking and sharing their posts) as we all appreciate acknowledgment of our contributions.

In a recent dream, a certain man had been accused of a terrible crime. I was a member of a group whose reactions were highlighted in the dream. I decided not to hold malice or hatred toward the man during his trial. At the end of the dream, I decided the best thing to do would be to offer him a job–immediately if he was acquitted. If he was convicted, I would offer him a job after he was released from prison. The dream is about the power of forgiveness and how our willingness to extend grace to someone can change their life.

One night, I had a dream where I met people who had undiagnosed mental illness that manifested as abdominal pain. Some of them became aware that they needed to be evaluated, but they still waited for a long time before they sought treatment. This was one of the first dreams I had that suggested physical symptoms of illness can be caused by emotional trauma.

In a dream I had in 2013, the power of suggestion was discussed and demonstrated. In the dream, I was highly skeptical toward the idea and had many objections. But a man pointed out the positive effects of the power of suggestion. He was patient with me while ignoring my objections. He focused on the idea that the mind and spirit have the ability to take things that are wrong and make them right—to bring life where there is death and light where there is darkness.

A few years ago, I had a dream where I saw a man who was successful at working miracles. A woman wanted to be, but she had poor results. I told her to try using the same words the man used. She said, "No one ever told me I should do that." She used the same words the man used and she had success. I would like to clarify the message of this dream.

Following a formula for healing and miracles is a recipe for failure. The point of the dream was that if we learn to emulate successful people, we will eventually have success. Not that we should copy them exactly, but that we should learn from them and adapt their methods to our personal style.

In 2011, my wife said she thought I had the potential to be an author. I had never considered writing as a career. Denise observed that I spent much of my free time writing. "All you do on your days off is write. Why not write for a living?" I though the idea was ludicrous. It's true that I wrote a great deal. On my days off work, I'd get up at sunrise, pour a cup of coffee and begin writing. Some days I'd correspond with friends on Facebook. Other days I'd write articles about healing. I love writing but I could not see myself as a professional writer. I'd planned to work as a paramedic as long as could. It had been my career for more than three decades. I no longer enjoyed the work, but I thought it was safe. Besides, I knew nothing about writing or publishing, and changing careers at my age seemed too great a risk. But Denise had a plan.

She once worked for a well-known book and magazine publisher and had experience creating cover designs and interior layouts. With her experience in publishing, and my natural love for writing, she believed I could become a successful author. All she had to do was harness my passion for writing and turn it in the right direction. Back then, I spent a lot of time engaging with other believers and writing about faith and healing on Facebook. She wanted to convince me to stop focusing so heavily on social media and direct my time toward writing a book manuscript.

One day, my son contacted me after having a dream about me. In the dream, I came to him excitedly and told him I had written my first book. He followed me into my bedroom where I showed him a book manuscript that was more than 1,000 pages in length. He asked when I had time to write it. I told him I had finally gotten off Facebook.

The dream suggested that if I wanted to write a book, I needed to take a break from Facebook. I deactivated my account for a few months and wrote the draft of my first book. In the years that followed, I've found it necessary to abstain from social media for months at a time when I want to finish a manuscript. I would have known none of this had it not been for a clever wife and a wise God who spoke to my son through a dream.

Around this time, I had many dreams about writing and publishing. In one dream, I had a long conversation about several terms that are used in publishing. A couple of words were discussed that had similar meanings but they were not exactly the same. The point of the discussion was to clarify these terms and remove ambiguity. As we've developed our publishing business, it has been extremely important to pay close attention to details.

Provision

When the Israelites were in the wilderness for 40 years, God took care of their needs. Their clothing did not wear out. Water came from a rock, and manna materialized on the ground every day. On that theme, years ago, my wife had a dream where she came out of a store, and the ground was covered with money. Dreams like this one symbolize God's willingness to meet all of our needs. We've learned that the key to receiving His provision is obeying the instruction He gives us.

In a dream I had after I first began publishing books, I was earning income that was held in an account. Periodically, an alarm would sound. At first, I didn't know what the alarm was for, but I learned that I had to transfer funds out of the account. At first, I only transferred a portion but eventually, I realized I had to transfer the entire balance when I was alerted. This happened regularly throughout the dream. Many people fear that they can't make a living as a writer. This dream confirmed that if I continued writing books, I would continue earning money.

Protection

I've been amazed at how God has protected me over the years. Many times, His protection has been disclosed in dreams. A friend once had a dream that they were observing activities at my house. They noticed two people sitting in a car parked on the street near my home. They knew these people had evil motives. They had been hired to surveil me. After watching my house for some time, they concluded I had purchased a sophisticated security system and drove away. In the dream, my friend saw four large angels watching over my property. Dreams like this one reveal how God protects us.

> *The name of the LORD is a strong tower;*
> *The righteous run to it and are safe.*
> PROV 18:10

Creativity

God is a Creator. He loves helping us create works of art, music and literature. He's interested in the things that interest us. My wife is a painter. One year, on her birthday, she had a dream where she was painting at an easel. As she worked, she noticed that occasionally, large drops of red paint were mysteriously splattering on the wall to the left of her canvas. She looked up, trying to find the source of the splatter. Then she looked to the left and saw a fantastically expressive portrait of Jesus being painted on the wall in red. In the dream, she knew Jesus was the one painting the large portrait of himself with big, bold brushstrokes. It was a great encouragement to her.

I once received the entire text of a short story in a dream. Not long ago, I received the storyline of a science fiction trilogy in a dream. There is no limit to the creative inspiration we can receive through dreams.

Intercession

Intercession can be defined as a prayer or petition to God on behalf of another. Sometimes a dream will be given in the night to direct you to pray for someone you don't know.

I once had a dream where I saw a car stranded on a snowy road. I knew there was a family inside the car and they needed help. I also knew God wasn't going to send help to them immediately. Instead, He would first reveal to them the reason they were there. Denise had been awake for several hours and woke me up because she heard me praying for someone while I was asleep. I was praying in the dream for the people in the car, but I wasn't aware I was praying out loud. After I awoke, we prayed together for the family to be rescued.

Training and Equipping

According to the Apostle Paul, the purpose of church leadership is to train and equip the saints for the work of ministry (Eph 4:11-12). My passion is teaching others how to live supernaturally. Many of my dreams involve training and equipping others.

In March of 2021, as I wrote this book, I had a dream illustrating this idea. In the dream, I observed firefighters and paramedics performing their duties with key pieces of equipment like oxygen tanks missing from their vehicles. They didn't notice the missing equipment, but I did. Soon after I noticed it was missing, so did they. Then the dream turned into an investigation to learn why the equipment was missing.

This dream is about missing equipment. Symbolically, it speaks of believers who are poorly trained and ill-equipped to handle the situations they face. My role as a leader is identifying these deficiencies and offering the needed training and equipping.

Character

It has been said that character is the person we are when no one is looking. God wants to develop in us impeccable character. He may speak to us about our character through dreams.

In 2012, I had a dream where I was at a shelter for ex-convicts. I spoke with residents to learn about their lives. I was then put in charge of their applications for permanent housing. If I didn't attend carefully to the details of their applications, they wouldn't have a place to live. I was tempted to be careless with their applications, thinking, "Why is this my problem?" But then, I talked with one woman about changing her behavior so she might avoid becoming a victim of sexual assault.

Chapter four in the book of Genesis contains the story of Cain and Abel. Cain became so jealous of his brother, Abel, that he killed him. Afterward, when God asked where Abel was, Cain said he didn't know. He replied, "Am I my brother's keeper?"

When we view others with disdain or contempt, we become like Cain. Godly character helps us see every life as valuable, and God will help us develop this kind of character.

Promotion

Genesis chapter 40 records the story of two of Pharaoh's servants and their dreams. After being thrown in prison, a butler dreamed he was serving Pharaoh again. Joseph interpreted the dream as a sign that he would be restored to his previous position.

In October of 2008, I had a dream where I was a high-ranking official in a city. The city was surrounded by vast countryside; its boundaries were well defined like those of a medieval village. I attended council meetings and planning sessions and voted on various measures. In the meetings, as someone was introduced to speak on an issue, they were given no political affiliation. Instead, they were announced by their spiritual affiliation. Some were witches or warlocks, others were Buddhists or Muslims, and still others were apostles or prophets. Nothing ever happened in these meetings that surprised me. I was always given information in advance about the matters to be discussed and the voting. I knew how each person would vote on a matter before they cast their vote. This dream suggested that a role had been prepared for me in a spiritual community that carried a measure of authority and that the position would have a prophetic component.

Destiny

Our divine destiny is the purpose for which God created us. It isn't just what we do; it's who we are at the core of our being. God will reveal our destiny in dreams. The question is whether we have the courage to pursue it.

On September 11th, 2011, I had a dream where I was sitting in a classroom having been invited by the instructor. Not long after taking a seat, the instructor introduced me and asked me to teach a class on healing. I frequently have dreams about healing and teaching because they're part of my destiny. I also have dreams about writing as it is through writing that I teach others.

Some know their divine destiny but they forgo opportunities to manifest it believing they can't make a living at it. Your destiny is closely tied to your greatest passion. If time and money were no object, and you could do anything you wanted, what would it be? Chances are, the answer to this question is related to your divine destiny. I never considered writing professionally; I didn't think I could make a living from it. After decades of ignoring my destiny, I'm finally living it.

CHAPTER FIFTEEN

Dream Complexity

SOME DREAMS ARE CONSTRUCTED USING a simple pattern. I know a man who had a dream where he met a friend who had recently died. The one who had died was a gifted preacher. He led many people to God. After seeing this departed saint appear in the dream, the man walked away, but his friend got his attention and tossed him a fish, which he caught. He then threw him a second and third fish, which he also caught. The interpretation is found in the gospel of Matthew. Jesus chose fishermen as His disciples. Being familiar with catching fish, He explained that if they followed Him, he would teach them to catch people. In the verse below, Jesus used the fishing metaphor to illustrate how they would draw people into a relationship with Him.

> *Then He said to them, "Follow Me, and I will make you fishers of men."*
> MATT. 4:19

In the dream, the man caught fish thrown to him by a friend who had brought people into the kingdom. The dream was a reminder that he had a similar calling.

When I was first learning dream interpretation, I had a dream where I used a computer to register for a prophetic conference in Corpus Christi, Texas. I assumed the dream was to be interpreted literally and spent the next week searching the internet for this conference. I didn't find it. Then one day, I asked God what the dream meant and heard a thought: Corpus Christi is Latin for "the body of Christ." Then it became clear. The prophetic conference in the dream spoke of prophecy as it related to me, personally. The city Corpus Christi symbolized the body of Christ i.e., the church. I wasn't supposed to go to a conference in Texas. I had a prophetic gift to be used for the body of Christ.

One approach to dream interpretation is to decode the meaning of each color, name, building, number, or vehicle, individually. Once you have an idea of what each symbol means, you construct a cohesive message. Since most symbols can have either a positive or negative meaning, an emotion felt in the dream and the flow of action will direct the interpretation. Let's look at a complex symbolic dream and interpret each symbol one by one.

In March of 2009, I had a dream of climbing a mountain with a group of people. We walked through a field of large boulders. As I watched one boulder, it suddenly rose up. Then, a boulder shifted a few feet to the left and crashed into another boulder. That collision displaced a massive rock. As I continued climbing, another large rock suddenly moved upward. I didn't notice, but I was carrying a container of water. As this rock raised up, the container of water was lifted over my head, and spilled on the person walking behind me. To my surprise, that person was Dutch Sheets. Dutch is a Christian leader who teaches on the kingdom of God from a prophetic perspective. He's wasn't hurt. He was laughing and let me know everything was okay. Now, let's interpret the elements of this dream one at a time.

Jesus is often symbolized in the Bible as a rock. "The stone that the builders rejected will become the chief cornerstone." Water often represents the Holy Spirit. On the day of Pentecost, the Holy Spirit was "poured out" on the disciples who gathered in the upper room. In the psalms, the kingdom of God is portrayed as a mountain. In the dream, I explored a mountain with friends. If the mountain is the kingdom of God, then the dream speaks of believers exploring the mysteries of His kingdom. The "rock that was lifted up" is Jesus, who is found by those who explore God's kingdom. The shifting rocks might indicate a spiritual shift that would occur at a future time. Unknowingly pouring water over Dutch Sheets suggests a sudden outpouring of the Holy Spirit on church leaders.

I use this approach to interpret dreams with multiple symbolic elements. Although this process seems more mechanical than receiving a sudden interpretation from God, it still requires the Holy Spirit to confirm the correct interpretation of each symbol and the overall interpretation.

Multiple Scenes & Multiple Dreams

Typically, a dream with more than one scene conveys a message about a single subject. The first scene identifies the subject. Subsequent scenes provide additional information about that subject. Occasionally, you'll have two or three dreams in a single night. Sometimes, multiple dreams in one night speak to the same issue. In these cases, the first dream establishes the subject, while subsequent dreams provide the details.

I often have dreams about a single subject over several days or a couple of weeks. In these dreams, the subject is established in the first dream, and the ones that follow provide more information on that subject. If you're having difficulty interpreting a particular dream, ask yourself if it might be related to a previous dream—one you've already interpreted.

Dreams in series are like the chapters of a book. If you follow them, they tell a story. Recording your dreams and reviewing them from time to time can help you see the big picture. More often than not, the story being conveyed is about the dreamer. We may have multiple dreams about the same subject over a span of time, but not everyone does. Some dreamers will have multiple dreams on the same night that are about different subjects. Initially, you may find it difficult to determine if sequential dreams are related, but it becomes easier with practice.

Is There a "Right" Interpretation?

If I were to visit an art museum with you, we would see various paintings, prints, photographs, and sculptures. The meaning you assign to a work of art is not the same that I would give it. The meaning we take away from art is highly subjective. A thousand people can listen to a speaker give a one-hour address and each listener will come away with a slightly different impression. Even in relatively objective matters, meaning tends to be subjective.

The people, places, colors, and objects that appear in dreams have many possible meanings depending on the context in which they appear. At some point, we will disagree over the interpretation of a dream, and that is exactly as it should be. Unlike crossword puzzles that are designed to have only one correct solution, dreams are constructed in such a way as to have multiple possible meanings. There may be agreement on the interpretation of a simple dream, but the more symbolic elements a dream has, the less likely there is to be consensus.

Dreams and visions are conveyed using symbolic elements, the meaning of which is personal to the dreamer. A dreamer who is familiar with their dream language is more likely to understand the meaning of their dreams than a stranger—even one who is skilled at interpretation. There is no way to verify the "correct" interpretation of a dream. Interpretations are subjective and as such, they're always open to debate.

Multiple Meanings

Some dreams have a way of speaking rather precisely to more than one issue. A dream may initially illustrate one issue in a dreamer's life, but later, it may apply to another.

Imagine having a dream where you move from your current home to a new home across town. If you have no plan to move when the dream is given, it may be interpreted symbolically. Two weeks after the dream, you learn that the company you work for is transferring you to an office across town. The dream would seem to have foreshadowed your transfer. Now let's say a year later, you move from your current home to a new home across town to be closer to where you work and the house you move to is the one you saw in the dream. This would not mean the first interpretation was wrong. It would rather suggest that the dream has two interpretations illustrating two realities—one symbolic and one literal.

Recurring Dreams

If we receive the same dream more than once, it's often because God intends to teach us something through successive lessons. Sometimes we'll receive the same dream multiple times; in other cases, a dream will change slightly each time. God instructs us about important issues through recurring dreams.

A friend who is an avid dreamer had a series of dreams over the span of time. In the first dream, she faced a frightening opponent who quickly killed her. In the next dream, she faced off against the same opponent, but this time, she looked around and found an ineffective weapon. She raised it against the opponent but was soon killed. The dreams continued in this way, and in each one, she found a slightly more effective weapon. Finally, in one dream, she pulled out a light saber like those used in the Star Wars films and used it to kill her opponent. That was the last dream she had of that kind. My friend realized God was warning her that she was ill-equipped for spiritual warfare. During the time she had these dreams, she learned to use spiritual weapons. Her progress was illustrated as the acquisition of more effective weapons. The final dream confirmed she had learned enough to wage spiritual warfare wisely.

Over the span of about ten years, I had a series of recurring dreams; the setting was an actual place where I once worked. When I was employed there, the management team was corrupt to the core. Co-workers who broke the law were protected by management—and anyone who questioned the status quo was harassed and threatened with violence. I clashed with these people the entire time I worked there.

After finding another job, I had dreams where I was working for this employer. Each dream showed negative interactions with former co-workers. I felt frustrated, hopeless, confused, and angry. One day it occurred to me that God wanted me to deal with the emotional trauma I suffered while working there. After submitting myself to the emotional healing process, the dreams changed. In a recent dream, I was with the manager in his office. I saw him as a clownish character, and he knew that I saw him this way. Filled with embarrassment, he tried to hide from me. Other co-workers I previously had negative feelings toward acted in a similar way. Rather than intimidating me, they tried to hide from me. The script had been flipped. Dishonesty and intimidation were exposed, and its perpetrators went scurrying for cover. These dreams motivated me to forgive them and seek emotional healing.

A Dream within a Dream

Occasionally, you may have what is referred to as a dream within a dream. Typically, the dreamer has what appears to be a normal dream and then—in that dream—they dream that they have another dream. The second dream does not have to be about a particular subject or person. The purpose for receiving a dream within a dream is similar to that of receiving the same dream twice. It is to emphasize the importance of the second dream. What may appear on the surface to be a normal dream, is, in fact, a highly important matter. God highlights the issue by nesting one dream inside another.

Interpretations Locked in Time

Since God gives the interpretation of dreams, we might wonder if there are times when He would not provide an interpretation. Most dreams can be interpreted soon after they're given, but not all of them can. After an angel had revealed many incredible things to the prophet Daniel, he then told him some of the revelation he'd received was not intended to be understood at the present time.

> *"But you, Daniel, shut up the words, and seal the book until the time of the end; many shall run to and fro, and knowledge shall increase."*
> DAN 12:4

For various reasons, the meaning of a dream or vision may be locked until an appointed time. Nothing we do will pry loose the interpretation prematurely. God may choose not to release an interpretation for reasons of operational security. In the military, if sensitive information is disclosed to an enemy, it can result in the failure of an operation or the death of operators. For that reason, the disclosure of sensitive information is limited to people who need to know and those who have the proper security clearance. Sometimes, God intends to bring an event to pass but if the details are revealed, our efforts to cooperate (even though well-intended) can ruin His plan. For that reason, He may show you a glimpse of a future event and nothing more. Then, at the right time, more understanding may be given to allow you to assist in bringing the event to pass, or to show that you were given advance notice.

In August of 2016, I had a dream where I watched Donald Trump release vast amounts of sensitive information over the internet to anyone who wanted it. I picked up much of what he released and shared it with people in my network. The information came from sources that would not normally divulge such secrets. It pertained mostly to finance and politics. These secrets had long enabled the political and economic ruling class to remain in power. If word ever got out about what the elites were doing behind closed doors, there would be consequences. In the dream, Trump made all of this information available to the public.

I was not a supporter of Trump at the time I received this dream. I was not sure what the dream meant. However, over a year later, a military intelligence operation began that awakened people to the realities of corruption. The evidence of corruption was made available to the public. In January of 2018, I began posting regular messages on social media explaining the relevance of the information. The operation became a global movement and created considerable controversy. Eventually, people questioned whether I should be involved in this movement. In the summer of 2018, I finally understood the dream from 2016. That dream confirmed that I was to be involved in an operation I would not know about until more than a year later.

Sometimes, the entire meaning of a dream will be given instantly, other times it will be given in parts. God may give us insight into the meaning of one symbol, while the others remain a mystery. Keeping the dream at the forefront of your mind will help bring further under-standing. Sometimes, as I ponder the scenes of a dream over several weeks, the meaning will gradually come to me. We don't need to be in a rush or force an interpretation. If we record our dreams and review them periodically, we will eventually understand them.

CHAPTER SIXTEEN

Conceptual Dreams

IN DREAMS, GOD MAY SYMBOLICALLY portray personal matters in the function, color, or size of an object like a house or automobile. In these dreams, you see the object. You may walk inside the house or drive the car. I often have dreams where I do not see a house or car, but the idea of one is represented abstractly.

When I first had these dreams, I had difficulty explaining them to others. Without sounding like a lunatic, how does one say, "I was shown the idea of a house, but I did not see the house itself?" A friend will naturally ask, "What do I mean by *the idea* of a house?

If we were to have a conversation about my house, I could use the words "my house" to indicate the house in which I presently live. The words "my house" represent the *idea* or *concept* of my house. You would understand my intent without needing to see the house itself.

That is what I mean by "the idea" of a house. I mean my house as an abstract concept as opposed to a concrete object.

In dreams, concrete objects are not always shown. Sometimes, an object or person is presented as an abstract idea. In the dream where I spoke with C.S. Lewis, I did not see Lewis himself. I knew that I was in his presence, the way we know things in dreams.

Imagine having a dream where you're standing before a wooded landscape watching trees clapping their branches the way humans clap their hands. This verse from the book of Isaiah would help with the interpretation.

> *"For you shall go out with joy,*
> *And be led out with peace;*
> *The mountains and the hills*
> *Shall break forth into singing before you,*
> *And all the trees of the field shall clap their hands.*
> ISA 55:12

We know that trees do not clap their hands. In this passage, the prophet used the literary tool of personification to give human attributes to a non-human subject. God often illustrates concepts in this way. Now imagine having a dream where you know you're standing before a wooded landscape, and you know the trees are clapping their branches. You do not see the trees, but you know they are present, and you know what they are doing.

I refer to these dreams as "conceptual" or "abstract" dreams. The objects themselves are not present, but an abstract concept is presented. If the concept presented in the dream is given human qualities, it might be described as a "personification" dream. God recently gave me one of these dreams.

In the dream, I knew the concept of a house was being presented. I did not see a house, but I knew that the idea of one was being illustrated. One particular house was for sale, and I knew that it could be given human personality traits. It could have a serious demeanor or a sarcastic attitude. The value of the house changed with its personality. If it had a marvelous sense of humor, its price increased. If it had a bitter personality, the price decreased. I saw several examples of how this house's personality could change and how the change affected its price.

One may question whether an automobile or house represents the personality traits of the dreamer. When an inanimate object takes on human characteristics, a more compelling argument is made that the dream reveals matters of the dreamer's personal life. In the dream I used as an example, God showed me that our personality has a value to our community. Some personality types are valued more, while others are valued less. Our disposition is a choice we make. The one we choose determines the value our community places on us.

I sometimes have dreams where the idea of a business is presented, but I don't see the business itself. I don't know the owner or the type of business being conducted. But in these dreams, I'm shown their plan to market a new product, reach a new audience or launch a new technology. The technology, product, or audience under consideration is usually an abstract concept. The concept being mentioned may sound foreign to the dreamer, but the interpretation is simple. Just as an unknown person can be a better version of the dreamer, an unknown business can represent the dreamer's business. The concepts illustrated in the dream can usually be applied to a situation in the dreamer's life. Strategies and tactics for successful business management are often revealed in conceptual dreams.

Whether a car, a house, or a business, an abstract concept presented in a dream usually represents some aspect of the dreamer's life just as it would if the object itself appeared.

Some dreams are purely spiritual, to the point where our soul perceives nothing about them at all. I had one of these dreams a few years ago. In it, I seemed to be in a classroom setting. I say "seemed" because I did not sense the classroom itself. I did not see it or an instructor. The only thing I was conscious of was that I was learning. When I awoke, I was aware that I had been learning, but I had no recollection of the cnvironment, the instructor, or the subject. It seemed as if I had been in a classroom the entire night. I inferred that I must have experienced a spiritual event—a lesson my spirit had participated in—one to which my mind was not privy. It can be frustrating waking from such an experience and remembering nothing, but in many cases, the lesson is intended only for our spirit and not our soul.

A few months after having this experience, I spoke with a friend who shared an experience she had. Her spirit had been visiting heaven regularly, and she had been receiving instruction from the spirit called Wisdom. (This spirit is the subject of several chapters in the book of Proverbs.) In this encounter, my friend spoke with Wisdom near a cliff that overlooked an amphitheater in heaven. Wisdom told her the amphitheater was used as a classroom, and the Apostle John was teaching that day. My friend looked down into the amphitheater and saw several people she recognized—one of them was me. I then told her about the dream where my spirit seemed to be learning the entire night. It was quite a coincidence.

Conceptual dreams may be difficult to understand if our mind is not accustomed to thinking in abstract terms. We may dismiss them because they seem illogical, but dreams defy the conventions of human logic. The wisdom of God is far more sublime than that of men. We must adjust our thinking if we hope to understand the language of heaven.

CHAPTER SEVENTEEN

Dreams of Future Events

THE BIBLE IS FILLED WITH passages foreshadowing events that would happen centuries in the future. Over three hundred pertain to the coming of Jesus as the Messiah.

> *Surely the Lord God does nothing, unless He reveals His secret to*
> *His servants the prophets.*
> AMOS 3:7

When God reveals the future to His servants, He does so in a peculiar way. The events themselves are often shrouded in symbolism, and the timing is seldom given.

God reveals future events both personal and global in scope. I've had dreams where I was transporting a patient in my ambulance, and a few days later, I transported the same person exactly as I had seen in the dream. The purpose of these dreams is personal. In most cases, God wanted me to know that a particular transport would be out of the ordinary, and I needed to anticipate certain events happening. Sometimes, the events unfolded exactly as I saw them in a dream; other times, they did not. Future events, as they're portrayed in dreams, are not always predictive in nature. They do not always show us what *will* happen. Sometimes, they reveal what *might* happen, depending on the will of the parties involved.

Years ago, I had a series of dreams about a nurse I frequently saw at a hospital. She had health problems, and I wanted her to be healed, but I was unsure if *she* wanted to be healed. In the dreams, God showed me the evil spirits that opposed her healing. He also told me that He wanted her healed. Two parties wanted her healed—God and me. One faction did not want her healed (the demons). The will of the individual who needed healing was unknown. Who would ultimately prevail was never shown to me. Healing is a complicated matter; you have the will of four entities to consider, all of whom are battling for their own version of victory.

Events in our lives happen on a timeline, but they are not under the control of a single entity. You have some idea of how you want your life to play out. But the decisions of others affect the events of your life. You might anticipate working a job for many years, and then someone steps off a plane carrying a virus, and everything changes. You might see yourself in a relationship for life until your fiancée dumps you. You might envision living to the age of 90 in excellent health, but a driver who runs a red light can forever alter your plans.

God may show us possible future events in dreams, but a definite, unalterable future is seldom given. Many times, we're shown a desire—what someone wants to happen, but not what *will* happen. Other times, we're shown the plans of God's enemies. We see a city destroyed, a stock market collapse, an assassination, the death of a loved one. These scenes usually reveal the desires of evil spirits, but they're not written in stone.

Sometimes, God shows us His desires, but not the final outcome. He always has a positive plan in mind for any situation, but His plan may not come to pass. I'm certain He would have preferred Joseph Stalin not rise to power and kill the people he did, but evil beings had other plans. God honors free will as well as prayer.

Recently, I listened to a man share his dreams about current events and then explain that the dreams meant we only had a few months before an oppressive global government would be ushered in and the financial markets would collapse. The man placed a short timeline (a few months) on his predictions, which have not come to pass. As I listened to him describe his dreams, it was apparent that he had been shown the plans of the kingdom of darkness. He assumed he had been shown God's plans, which he thought could not be altered. This caused him to make dire predictions about the future.

One problem with understanding future events stems from our worldview. Our view of the future is unconsciously imposed on our interpretation of dreams. If our view is not God's view, we'll misinterpret them. Many people believe the earth is destined to become engulfed in ever more devastating wars. One biblical view of the future supports this idea, but others do not. It's impossible to say with certainty which (if any) view of the future is correct. When a dream reveals the enemy's plan to start a war, the dreamer might mistakenly take it as God's inescapable will and come into agreement with it. Generally, when we're shown some tragedy in a dream, God is not showing us a predetermined future. He's showing us the desire of His enemy, and He expects us to oppose it. Our task is to stand in faith and declare authoritatively that it will not come to pass.

One way God illustrates personal change is through dreams of natural disasters. Tornadoes, floods, volcanoes, earthquakes, and storms, when seen in dreams, can depict sudden, dramatic changes in life. A new job, a move across the country, a death in the family or the loss of a business can be represented as a natural disaster. Be cautious when predicting a literal natural disaster after having one of these dreams. They are almost always symbolic. More importantly, they may portend changes you need to prepare for.

When you examine the prophetic passages of scripture, you'll find that only rarely is a time frame given for a prophecy to come to pass. In the few cases where that information is given—the birth of Jesus, for example—it's presented in such vague terms that only a few people recognized the approaching fulfillment. God often shows us the "what" but seldom shows us the "when." We may be shown who is involved in a future event or where it will happen, but the timing is usually not given. Even when we're given what we believe is the timing, it may not come to pass at the time or in the way we expect.

If you're given dreams of future events, they will likely pertain to a limited number of subjects over which you have authority or spiritual jurisdiction. Jeremiah prophesied almost exclusively about the nation of Israel, as did many of the Old Testament prophets. King Nebuchadnezzar's dreams were about his kingdom and the ones that followed. Pharaoh's dreams pertained to Egypt. Our dreams will usually pertain to us or our community. There may be certain topics about which God gives us understanding, but the subject matter of our dreams can change over time. For years, I had dreams about healing, but in 2016, most of my dreams turned to current events and politics. This wasn't my doing. The change in subject matter was at God's discretion.

Sometimes, we'll be shown a future event in a dream and have to guess as to how it should be interpreted or applied. Around the time of the U.S. 2020 presidential election, I received a number of dreams, nearly all of which related to the election. In one dream, I consoled people outside a church building. I knew these individuals had turned their backs on God years earlier and were returning to Him. One by one, they came to me, put their head on my shoulder, and cried. They were broken-hearted, and I offered a shoulder to cry on.

Although nothing in the dream spoke of it, because other dreams I'd had at that time were about the election, I inferred that this dream was too. I was concerned that if the election did not go the way people anticipated, people would be devastated. Leaders like me would then need to console them. And that is precisely what happened.

My first dream from God (as an adult) came on the night of August 8th, 2008 (8/8/08). Exactly eight years later, on August 8th, 2016, my wife and I both had dreams about then-candidate Donald Trump. I'm not at liberty to share my wife's dream, but I will share its interpretation after I share my dream.

On the night we had our dreams, we listened to a speech Trump gave to Detroit business leaders. In the speech, he outlined his plan for economic recovery. He planned to erase America's trade deficit, create a trade surplus, and bring millions of jobs back to America. After listening to the speech, we went to bed.

In my dream, I saw something like a poll asking people to express their political preference. I expressed a preference for Trump and stepped into what seemed like another dimension where everyone had the best of everything. We lived in blessing and prosperity of every kind imaginable. There was no poverty or sickness. No one was homeless. It seemed as if heaven had come to earth. It was, in a word—lavish. My wife's dream also showed that those who aligned with Trump would experience the best that life has to offer. The last thought I had before going to sleep that night was how God had promised the Israelites a land flowing with milk and honey. It was a place of abundance. God offered them a lavish lifestyle, if only they would receive it. In my dream, it seemed as if we, the people, were offered a similar opportunity.

Then in 2016, U.S. citizens *did* elect candidate Trump as President. He started to put the country on a path to recovery and prosperity. At that point, the dreams looked to be a glimpse into our immediate future as a society. But with the global health scare, and the election of 2020, the progress of the Trump years began to slip away.

It's possible that God merely showed me His desire for our nation and nothing more. He may not have shown me what *will* be, but what *could have* been. Did Joe Biden's inauguration forever cancel the possibility of this future? It's impossible to say. How long should I wait before I conclude that it won't happen? Five years? Twenty years? If it doesn't happen this year, some will say it will never happen. Again, the matter of timing comes into play. God gave me no indication as to when it will happen. Perhaps it will never come to pass, but I choose to believe it will. If any future God shows us is to become a reality, we must do the work required to manifest it. God doesn't sovereignly bring change to our culture without our participation. He shows us possibilities; we decide if we want them.

Part Three

CHAPTER EIGHTEEN

Putting Dreams into Action

NOW THAT WE'VE LEARNED TO interpret dreams, it's time to put them into action. This is where the rubber of dreams meets the road of reality. Dreams are given to motivate us to live differently—to change us. Our outward behavior changes when our inner thought life is transformed. The messages that follow will challenge you to consider whether your dreams are asking you to live differently than you are at present.

Advice on Sharing Dreams

Most people don't share their private emails with friends. Communication between two people is expected to be held in confidence. The same principle applies to sharing dreams. God gives us personal dreams to convey information important to us, but not to others. When Joseph shared a couple of dreams with his family, it didn't go well.

Joseph had a dream, and when he told it to his brothers... He said to them, "Listen to this dream I had: We were binding sheaves of grain out in the field when suddenly my sheaf rose and stood upright, while your sheaves gathered around mine and bowed down to it."

His brothers said to him, "Do you intend to reign over us? Will you actually rule us?" And they hated him all the more because of his dream and what he had said.

Then he had another dream, and he told it to his brothers. "Listen," he said, "I had another dream, and this time the sun and moon and eleven stars were bowing down to me."

When he told his father as well as his brothers, his father rebuked him and said, "What is this dream you had? Will your mother and I and your brothers actually come and bow down to the ground before you?" His brothers were jealous of him, but his father kept the matter in mind.

GEN 37:5-11

Some dreams reveal information about people who see you as an adversary. You may be unaware that they perceive you this way, and you may incorrectly assume they won't understand your dream. If they see you as a threat, either personally or in business, the dream could cause them to take action against you. For that reason, it is wise to keep personal dreams to yourself.

Having said that, I share many of my dreams with my wife because she is not my adversary. She loves me, and she benefits from the information in my dreams.

I share some dreams on social media, but I'm very selective. I will not share a dream if I don't know (or suspect I know) what it means. I won't share a dream if it provides potentially valuable information to someone who views me as an enemy. I'll only share a dream publicly if it has the potential to help those who hear and understand it. Learning which dreams to share and which to keep to yourself is a delicate matter. Like everything, you'll get better with experience.

The Wake-up Call

In a previous chapter, I suggested writing down the time if you happen to look at a clock when you wake in the night from the dream. Some years ago, I awoke from a dream at exactly 4:20, three nights in a row. I'm not sure why I looked at my clock each night, but I did. It seemed odd that I awoke at the same time. I thought perhaps God was pointing me to a scripture verse. I searched each book of the Bible for ones with a fourth chapter and twentieth verse, looking for one that spoke to my spirit. At the time, I had been wrestling with whether the stories I'd published about the miracles I had seen were more about building my ego or if I intended to give credit to God. As I searched the scriptures, I smiled when I came to the book of Acts. In chapter three, Peter and John had just healed a lame man in the name of Jesus. In chapter four, word got out, and many people became believers. When the religious leaders warned Peter and John not to preach in the name of Jesus, this was their response:

> *But Peter and John answered and said to them, "Whether it is right in the sight of God to listen to you more than to God, you judge. For we cannot but speak the things which we have seen and heard."*
> ACTS 4:19-20

Waking at 4:20 confirmed that I had a duty to tell people the things God had done through me. If I struggled with pride, that was my problem. It did not negate my responsibility to tell others about Jesus.

Not long after I had this experience, my wife had a similar one. She received a prophetic word from a trusted friend that she was in a season of rest but had difficulty believing it. She'd been feeling a great deal of stress during this so-called season of rest and found herself waking up at 4:10 every morning for no apparent reason. After this happened several days in a row, she thought she might ask God what He was trying to tell her. A thought then came to mind pointing her to the book of Hebrews.

> *"For he who has entered His rest has himself also ceased from his works as God did from His."*
> HEB 4:10

Prophetic Ministry

Not everyone is called to operate in a prophetic capacity, but I am, and so are many of my friends. This section provides tips on how dreams and visions can help you function more effectively if you're called to a prophetic ministry.

Although the dreams of most people tend to focus on *them*, prophetic ministers often have dreams about *others*. The purpose of these dreams is to convey information about a specific person or group to assist the dreamer in their ministry.

Dreams, where others are the main focus, are different from dreams about yourself. In dreams where you are the focus, you are typically present and play a role. In dreams where another person is the focus, the dreamer is usually not present, and if they are, they play no significant part.

I have many dreams about others. In them, I'm an invisible observer. I watch the actions that take place, listen to conversations, and note what is said. Sometimes, I'm given insights into the thoughts of others, but no one interacts with me or even notices I'm there.

A prophetic intercessor may have a dream where they're watching their pastor deliver a message to his congregation. Suddenly, he's surrounded by snakes that are biting him. The dreamer is an observer, and no one notices them. This dream is not about the dreamer but the pastor. It's a warning that he's facing opposition, and the dreamer should pray for him.

During his Presidency, many people had dreams showing the assassination (or attempted assassination) of Donald Trump. It would be easy to assume that God had given such dreams as a sign that he would be killed in office. Dreams of this nature rarely point to definite future events. More often, they expose the plan of an enemy that can be prevented through prayer and intercession. These dreams are about the leader portrayed in them. They're given to motivate us to pray and intercede on their behalf so that the event that was revealed does not come to pass.

A similar situation arises when we have dreams of natural disasters. Prophetic people frequently have dreams of floods, earthquakes, tsunamis, tornadoes, and other cataclysmic events. Some interpret these dreams literally, but as we know, most dreams are intended to be interpreted symbolically. Between 2008 and 2013, many prophets prophesied that here would soon be devastating earthquakes on the western coast of the United States. These quakes did not manifest. It's possible the earthquakes they saw were warnings of dramatic changes coming in society—something that has certainly happened on the west coast over the last ten years. It's equally possible these dreams spoke of personal changes in the lives of the dreamers.

In January of 2009, I had a dream where I watched from space as the earth entered an energy field that caused widespread destruction on the surface of the planet. I watched the Seattle space needle become engulfed in a blazing inferno. Other buildings also burned up. Roads and brick structures melted into liquid as the wave of energy destroyed everything man had built. It would be difficult to interpret this dream literally, but it may have foreshadowed the dramatic societal changes that have rocked Seattle between 2019 and 2021. Let's consider another possibility.

If you believe the end of the earth is fast approaching, you could interpret this dream as a harbinger of the end of days. But as I watched in awe, a couple of verses from Peter's second epistle were brought to my attention:

> *But the day of the Lord will come as a thief in the night, in which the heavens will pass away with a great noise, and the elements will melt with fervent heat; both the earth and the works that are in it will be burned up. Therefore, since all these things will be dissolved, what manner of persons ought you to be in holy conduct and godliness?*
> 2 PET 3:10-11

While this passage does mention the destruction of the earth, the point Peter made was that we ought to live out our lives in godly character. The dream was a reminder, not about the end of the world, but to walk circumspectly and not be caught up in the schemes of the enemy.

In 2008, I had a dream where I was at the house of a friend named Jim. In the first scene of the dream, we were installing the drive shaft of a car and talking with his friend as we worked. In the second scene, we were on top of his house, repairing his roof. He was on one part of the roof with his friend, nailing shingles while I worked on the adjacent part. I saw Jim about a week after having the dream and told him about it. He was shocked. It turns out he was in his shop the day I had the dream fixing his son's car. Three days later, the roof of his house collapsed in a storm. The point of the dream was to show him that God is aware of his circumstances.

Years ago, I was connected to many people on Facebook who operated in divine healing. One group of healers was antagonistic toward me because they disagreed with my views on a couple of minor issues. After that group had grown in popularity and then self-destructed through infighting, I had dreams about the group's two most prominent leaders. In one dream, I saw a man I'll call Frank go through a long period of silence on social media. He spent his time with God. Years later, he had a very successful ministry of raising the dead. I messaged him and shared the dream, which he received with gratitude. I had a similar dream about the other leader. I sent him a message explaining the dream, and he received it in humility.

I receive and provide prophetic direction to others because I asked God for this ministry. I once heard Bob Jones explain that part of his calling was providing direction to struggling leaders. Bob received dreams that provided direction. After he received a dream, he would contact the person he saw in it and deliver a message. I thought it was a wonderful ministry, so I asked God if I could have similar opportunities. I want to provide a word of caution about giving direction to others.

I rarely give my opinion when it is not asked for. Even my grown children know that if they want my advice, they must ask for it. People do not value or heed advice that is not wanted. I refrain from offering my opinion to others until and unless I've established a relationship of trust with them, and they've asked for my opinion. Ministry flows through relationships. The stronger the relationship, the more you will be able to minister to someone. Before you give a prophetic word to a stranger, you might consider establishing a relationship with them.

If they come to trust you, when you tell them what God has shown you, they'll be more likely to receive it. In the case where I shared dreams with the two men mentioned above, I had to wait months and show them I wanted their best and that I held no animosity toward them. When I sensed that they understood this, I was able to share the dreams about them, and just as importantly, they accepted them as God had intended.

Years ago, I was given a vision. In it, I saw a piece of aluminum that had been milled into a support for an airplane wing. A boy swung the piece of metal in a circle inside a large building. Suddenly, the piece of metal changed into an airplane wing, and continued flying in a circle. Next, it transformed into an airplane that continued slowly circling inside the building. Finally, it became a B-17 bomber. I watched as the bomber continued flying slowly in a tight circle inside a building that resembled a church.

God spoke to me about two things from this vision. One is the idea of momentum. From the beginning of the vision, the piece of aluminum had developed forward momentum and it never ceased once it began. Many people find it difficult to fulfill their destiny because they allow obstacles to slow them down. The vision emphasized that sustaining forward momentum is necessary for us to grow.

The second thing that struck me was the absurdity of a B-17 bomber flying inside a building. This was a church metaphor. God carefully shapes and transforms us into powerful weapons of warfare to be used against the kingdom of darkness, and we're content to operate inside a building we call the church. The spiritual battlefield is not found inside the walls of a building, but in the environment we inhabit every day of our lives. If we confine ourselves to a building, we inflict little damage to the kingdom of darkness.

Expectations

Noah had a fascinating ministry. We don't know how it was revealed that the earth would one day be flooded, but somehow, he knew. It had never rained in the known history of man, but for years, Noah warned everyone who would listen that torrential rain was coming.

They mocked him and called him crazy—until the day the rain came, and he sealed the door of the ark.

Although Noah knew *what* was coming, he didn't know *when* it was coming. God showed him the flood but gave no indication as to when it would arrive. Many people have had to walk back their prophetic declarations after a predicted event failed to materialize. I once prophesied an event to the best of my understanding, but it did not come to pass. At least not in the way I had expected.

Occasionally, an event God showed us will come to pass, but not in the way we expect. We may be completely unaware that it happened because we anticipated one thing while God did something else. There is no disappointment without expectation. In most cases, when our prophetic word goes sideways, it's not because we're a false prophet. It's because we had wrong expectations. When you give a prophetic word based on a dream or vision, and it doesn't come to pass as expected, ask the Holy Spirit where you went wrong. The most accurate prophetic ministers are the most teachable. Learn from your mistakes and try not to repeat them.

Joseph was called out of prison to interpret the dreams of Pharaoh. Because he correctly interpreted them, Egypt was saved. Prophetic ministry executed correctly can impact the fate of a nation. Not everyone will have a ministry with a national scope, but some will. It is an awesome responsibility and it is not to be taken lightly. One rises to the level of national influence when God finds them to be faithful in smaller responsibilities. If He has called you to a prophetic ministry, be consistent. Be transparent. Be reliable. If you carry out your assignment in humility, God may one day use you to impact your nation.

CHAPTER NINETEEN

Receiving Dreams

FOR 25 YEARS, I HAD not received a single dream. Not even one I had forgotten. I suspect God may have withheld my dreams for a specific reason. When we go without love for any length of time, our need for it intensifies. Absence makes the heart grow fonder. Those who dream regularly often say, "it was just a dream." This phrase captures the sentiment that when we dream frequently, one dream is no more valuable than the last hundred. But when you go 25 years without a single dream, each one you have carries significance. Perhaps God withheld my dreams so I would take each one seriously when I finally began dreaming.

My dream life seems to have been activated by a simple prayer my wife said over me. She had spent the weekend at a dream interpretation workshop hosted by a friend named Melody Paasch. Melody told Denise she could pray for me to have dreams since I did not dream. Denise came home and asked God to give me dreams. That night, I had my first dream as an adult. If you're not presently having dreams, find someone who is and have them pray for you to receive them.

Many people believe God chooses whom He sends dreams to and whom He does not. They believe we can do nothing to control the dreams we receive. Although we may not admit it, we suspect He may have favorites. If you're on the list of favorites, you get all the dreams you could ever want (lucky you). But if you're not on the list—you receive nothing. I believe God wants to give dreams and visions to everyone. And I suspect He tries to send them to all of us, but we may unknowingly prevent them from being delivered.

How can we prevent dreams from being delivered? The problem might best be explained by examining what are sometimes called the "spiritual laws," one of which is the law of sowing and reaping. It's explained in the Apostle Paul's second letter to the church in Corinth.

> *He who sows sparingly will also reap sparingly, and he who sows bountifully will also reap bountifully. So let each one give as he purposes in his heart, not grudgingly or of necessity; for God loves a cheerful giver.*
> 2 COR 9:6-7

The principle Paul explained is that if we give from a generous heart, we will receive abundantly from others. One action begets another, as long as the inciting action is rightly motivated. For it is the motive of our heart (in this example, generosity) that causes the reciprocating action.

Jesus explained another spiritual law that has to do with how we receive wisdom from God. It was His response when His disciples asked why he taught in parables.

> *And the disciples came and said to Him, "Why do You speak to them in parables?"*
>
> *He answered and said to them, "Because it has been given to you to know the mysteries of the kingdom of heaven, but to them it has not been given. For whoever has, to him more will be given, and*

he will have abundance; but whoever does not have, even what he has will be taken away from him.
MATT 13:10-12

This comment was made in response to the scribes and Pharisees who had rejected Jesus' straightforward teaching. They didn't value divine revelation, so what little they had would be removed. But the disciples valued it and they received more. In the same way, if we value divine revelation like dreams, we will be given more of them. And the ones we have will reveal deeper truths. But if we do not treasure dreams, we will receive less of them. And the few we have will reveal less important truths. Our view of divine revelation determines both the quantity and quality of our dreams. This concept was illustrated in a dream I had in February of 2015.

In the dream, I was shown how God will speak to certain people through a limited number of symbolic messages. The limitation was necessary because of the individual's limited understanding. One example was given with a particular person. The revelation for them took the form of a long, thin pastry that they ate. It was the only thing for which they had an appetite. Their spiritual appetite restricted the revelation they could receive. This is not unlike the way a person who is fluent in five languages understands more of human culture than a person who only understands one. The restriction to our understanding is usually self-imposed.

We must also consider the matter of our will. Dreams come to our spirit and are viewed by our soul in our imagination. God does not control our spirit or soul. By exercising our will, we can choose to receive or reject revelation from God. Once we've decided not to receive dreams, God may try to send them, but our spirit will not receive them.

I have a friend who has been a believer for 40 years. He confided in me that he didn't have many dreams, and the few he did have were sexual in nature. He did not want these dreams, and as a result, he stopped having them for several months. He read my book *Seeing in the Spirit Made Simple* and came to my discussion about shutting down our imagination because of things we've seen that we don't like. It occurred to him that perhaps he had shut down his ability to receive dreams because he had ones he didn't like. He made a conscious decision to open his imagination. He wrote to me saying that since making this decision, he's had dreams every night, and so far, only one has been of a sexual nature.

If you're not receiving visions or dreams, you might consider whether you've shut down your imagination. If you have, simply verbalizing out loud that you want to receive revelation from God can open up the flow. When dreams and visions are received, if you see things you don't want to see (demonic dreams for example), remind the enemy that you're not his pawn. Tell him you will not receive any revelation from him. It's a simple application of the admonition from the Apostle James: "Resist the devil and he will flee from you." In the same way that you can shut down the flow of revelation from God, you can shut down the flow of revelation from evil spirits. If you resist the revelation the enemy sends, it will gradually subside and, over time, leave completely. And that brings us to the subject of nightmares.

Nightmares

It's my view that most dreams, including nightmares, are messages sent by spirit beings of one kind or another. The terrorizing effect of nightmares suggests they are not from God but evil spirits. Just as we ought not sit idly by and allow thieves to break into our house, we should not passively allow demons to terrorize us at night. In the same way we can refuse unwanted sexual dreams, we can refuse to receive nightmares. Resisting the work of evil spirits is a matter of exercising our God given authority. That authority was granted to us by Jesus:

Behold, I give you the authority to trample on serpents and scorpions, and over all the power of the enemy, and nothing shall by any means hurt you.
LUKE 10:19

One might ask, if we've been given authority over all the power of the enemy, why does it seem like the enemy has the upper hand? Many believers are not aware they've been given this authority and some who know they have it, don't know how to use it. Authority offers no advantage until it is exercised. Nightmares are a form of terrorism. In the same way a terrorist bomber wants to put fear in the minds of a population, evil spirits want us to live in fear. The way to deal with a terrorist is to deny them what they want. Fear is an emotion; living in fear is a choice. If you refuse to live in fear, the terrorist will find someone else to harass. "Resist the devil and He will flee from you," is an observation that evil spirits can be defeated by resisting their work. If we choose not to react in fear to nightmares, they will subside, since the evil spirit sending them won't get the outcome they desire.

The Culture We Create

I've noticed that as I spend time with certain people, their interests, talents, or gifts are transferred to me. Between 2008 and 2014, I spent much of my time in discussions with healers. The more time I spent with them, the more success I had in healing. I also became interested in prophecy and as I spent time with prophetic people, my own prophetic gift grew. My wife doesn't see herself as prophetically gifted, but when she's around those who are prophesying, the Spirit of prophecy comes over her and she operates in this gift. As Denise and I have spent time in the company of dreamers, the number of dreams we have and our understanding of them has increased.

This dynamic appears to solve the problem of a person's limited understanding, which I mentioned above. Poor understanding limits our ability to receive spiritual revelation like dreams and visions. To be more precise: part of the problem is our limited understanding—the other part is our limited level of *interest*. Being with those who have spiritual understanding and who operate from it, imparts a degree of understanding to us. But it also increases our interest in a subject and our capacity to receive revelation on that subject. As we immerse ourselves in a culture, the collective knowledge of the culture may be imparted to us as well as a heightened interest, effectively removing our self-imposed limitations.

This could be why God wants us to come together as a community regularly. Interacting with others provides opportunities for a community to grow spiritually. So, if you want to learn to heal, hang around healers. If you want to learn to prophesy, find out where the prophets are, and meet with them. If you desire to have more dreams, spend time with dreamers. The culture in which you immerse yourself will impact your experiences.

CHAPTER TWENTY

Ears to Hear

ONE OF MY GREATEST SHORTCOMINGS is my tendency to hold on to what I believe a little too tightly. I treasure my theological and political views, and on many issues, I don't have an open mind. Although being too open-minded can lead us into error, being too closed-minded can also work against us.

Many of my friends have embraced a particular view of the future after having read a book written by a well-known teacher. Although friends have repeatedly urged me to read this book, I've resisted. I've justified my obstinance by telling them I already know the writer's viewpoint. I've studied the subject. I know his arguments. I even engaged the author in a lengthy online discussion a few years ago and heard what he had to say. On this issue, I've had very little interest in hearing different views. And that's unfortunate. God speaks to me most when my mind is not made up on an issue. When my views have been cemented firmly in place, there's no room for dialogue. But when my views are flexible—when I have an open mind—there's room for instruction. If we want to be instructed by God, we must first admit we don't have the answers. As it turned out, I did come around to this man's way of thinking, but my mind was changed not by reading his book but through revelation I received from God.

The first step (for me) in receiving instruction from God is knowing what He wants to discuss. When I presume to know what's on His mind, I'm often wrong. On any given day, I don't know what He wants to teach me. When I want to find out what's on His agenda, I expose my mind to various subjects and let *Him* pick the ones that are most important to Him. Let me illustrate what that looks like.

When I first became interested in healing, I listened to messages by Todd White, Randy Clark, and others who had success in healing. After listening to one of these messages, I'd often have a dream where one of these men would appear and teach me something. The things that were on my mind were also on God's mind.

I will often have a discussion with someone during the day, and later that night, God will give me a dream. Sometimes, the conversation will continue in the dream. Other times, God will highlight something that was said or point out an aspect of the person's character that He wants me to understand.

A few years ago, I read Michael Van Vlymen's book on spiritual travel called, *Supernatural Transportation*. Bruce Allen wrote a book on the same subject. The night I began reading the book, Michael and Bruce visited me in a dream and gave me a message. These men are forerunners and have valuable experience with this subject. The fact that they gave me a message in a dream suggested that it was important for me to learn what I could from them. Michael's book answered a crucial question with which I was wrestling as I worked on my own book on this subject.

Sometimes, I expect confirmation, but God does not give it. Not long ago, I attended a meeting where a prophet spoke who usually provides detailed prophecies of the future. I was interested in hearing what he had to say, and I was certain God would confirm his message. (He nearly always does that for me through dreams, but He may confirm things for you in a different manner.) After listening to the prophet, I went to bed expecting to receive a dream of confirmation, but it never came. In fact, I haven't had confirmation of any of the revelation I've heard from this prophet. In this case, what was on my mind was not on God's mind.

The fact that God did not provide confirmation doesn't mean this man is a false prophet. He has a remarkable prophetic ministry. But it does suggest that his messages are not where God wants me to focus. This man happens to have a negative view of the future. God seldom confirms (for me) prophetic messages from a pessimistic viewpoint. I once held a negative view of the future. As a new Christian I was taught pre-millennial dispensationalism. Most adherents to this view believe the earth will soon be subjected to an oppressive global government. Although God has shown me some concerning future events, at present, my view of the future is optimistic. The change came when I set aside my own views and asked God to show me His. I've allowed my mind and spirit to come into agreement with the positive things He has shown me.

In the summer of 2016, God began highlighting political candidates in my dreams. In July of that year, the Republican Party held its National Convention. I listened to most of the speeches each night of the convention, and on three of the four nights, God gave me dreams about Donald Trump. I was not a Trump supporter when I began having dreams about him. But I had determined I would let God speak to me about the candidates. During the next four years, I received more than 100 dreams about President Trump. The dreams were given because I had an open mind.

On a typical day, I might be exposed to messages on ten different subjects. I read articles and books, watch videos, listen to podcasts, and interact with people in person and online. Then I go to sleep and let God speak about the issues that are important to Him. Sometimes He confirms a message I heard or read that day, but other times, He doesn't. Occasionally, He'll speak about something that was not on my mind that day.

If you want to know what God's view is on a particular issue, you may need to surrender your theological views, your political ideology, and your deeply held convictions. All of them can be misguided. If you're not having dreams about a particular subject, you might consider how rigid your views are on that matter. Give God permission to teach you the truth, and when He does, don't question it. Accept His perspective, and allow it to become yours.

CHAPTER TWENTY-ONE

The Path We Choose

DREAMS ARE WINDOWS TO A different life; glimpses of how we're living now compared with how we might live. If we take our dreams seriously, they will change us. God is perpetually calling us to an upgraded life—one that is different in every way from how we are living at the present. What does it mean to live differently? We can't always gauge what it might be like if we follow the instruction we receive from God in dreams. We're given hints, but the entire path isn't clearly revealed. The paths I might have chosen were explained to me one night in a dream.

In the dream, I spoke with someone about different types of terrain upon which we walk. I saw many different surfaces. Some were smooth. Others were rough. We talked about them and how there are different ways of traveling over each one and different results depending on the mode of travel we choose.

One approach was to simply walk, regardless of the surface. Another was to use a pair of roller blades. Throughout the dream, as different types of surfaces were shown, different modes of travel were demonstrated. I learned how to choose the best (most efficient) way to travel over each surface. As I drove to work with my wife the following day, we talked about the dream. The more we discussed it, the more insight we gained into what it meant.

The different surfaces upon which people walked represent how we might live our lives. A rough and bumpy surface represented a life filled with difficulty, while a smooth surface symbolized a life of ease. Each person walks one type of path or another. Some of the features of our path are out of our control. One has no control, for example, over the country in which one is born.

But some features of our path are ours to choose. Some choose to be peacemakers. Others chose to live in a way that makes them an adversary to others. Some choose to comply with the status quo. Others choose to be rebels. The choices we make dictate the kind of path we walk. Rebels create a bumpy path for themselves, while those who go along with the status quo choose a smooth one.

The goal in the dream was to find the right mode of travel across the different types of terrain. Wheels worked well on smooth surfaces, but they were not a good choice for rough surfaces. The best choice for a rough surface was walking.

At times, I've chosen to act like a maverick. I may have denied it at times, but it's true, and it was a choice I made. As a non-conformist, I created situations for myself that brought criticism and opposition. I couldn't understand why I received so much opposition, but in hindsight, it was the natural reaction to my rebellious attitude. The problem was that I chose to walk a path full of ruts, bumps, and potholes, but had not developed the spiritual maturity it takes to walk that path. Spiritual immaturity leaves us unable to respond graciously to harsh criticism. We don't recognize constructive criticism when it is given, so we react unkindly to all criticism. Godly rebels are different. They're less affected by criticism. They're convinced of their identity, confident in their mission, and unmoved by public opinion.

When I was young, I chose to walk the path of a rebel, but I was spiritually immature and was always offended. My views had not been established over time and were susceptible to manipulation and change. I didn't know my identity, so it changed from year to year, depending on my current interests. I had no idea what my mission, purpose, or destiny were. I'm not sure I knew what those words meant. I had chosen a path I was not equipped for. I wore roller blades when I needed a pair of hiking boots.

The dream was a parable. The point was that we ought to choose our path wisely and be sure we're equipped for the one we've chosen. Many of us are not equipped for the paths we're currently traveling. There are two solutions to this dilemma: We can choose to walk a different path—an easier one more suited to our current level of spiritual maturity. Choosing an easier (smoother) path would allow us to avoid the need for further training. The other option is receiving training and equipping to help us walk a more difficult path. Harder paths mean more resistance, but the rewards are greater. My books have one purpose—to train and equip people like you to navigate the difficult paths of life with the tools and attitude you need to succeed. I hope this book achieves that purpose. I pray that you will endeavor to follow your dreams, wherever they may lead.

Part Four

CHAPTER TWENTY-TWO

Dream Symbols

THIS CHAPTER IS A REFERENCE for those who wish to explore possible meanings of people, places and things that appear in dreams. Due to space constraints, it is not an exhaustive list of dream symbols, but commonly appearing items can be found herein. Consider these definitions to be suggestions rather than rules. Interpretations other than those provided in this chapter may be valid. Most symbolic subjects have both positive and negative interpretations. Generally, definitions will be listed for each word in order from most positive to most negative. Bible verses are provided as reference for most entries and may or may not correlate with the order in which definitions are listed. Bible verses are taken from the New King James Version unless otherwise noted.

··· A ···

Abandoned house: Barrenness; desolation. (Job 15:28.)

Abandoned road: Following one's own plans; stubbornness. (Jer 18:15.)

Acid: Bitterness; offense; carrying a grudge; sarcasm; hatred. (Acts 8:23; Heb 12:15.)

Adoption: Acceptance into God's family. (Rom 8:15.)

Adultery: Dishonoring marriage vows; sin; idolatry; pornography. (Ezek 23; James 4:4; Eccl 7:26; Prov 30:20; Matt 5:28.)

Aging: Wisdom; honor; death. (Deut 32:7.)

Aircraft carrier: Support of spiritual warfare.

Airliner: Large church congregation; ministry to many.

Airport: A place of departure; waiting to transition from one phase of life to another.

Alien (extraterrestrial): Literal being from another planet; foreigner; evil spirit or fallen angel; angelic messenger of God; believer; outcast; unbeliever. (Deut 24:14; Deut 28:43; 1 Chron 29:15; Eph 2:12; Heb 11:13; Heb 13:2.)

Alligator: Ancient one; evil spirit; devourer. (Isa 27:1.)

Almond: Watchful; fruitful. (Jer 1:11; Num 17:8.)

Aloe: Fragrance; healing; anointing. (Ps 45:8; Prov 7:17; John 19:39.)

Altar: Place of sacrifice or slaughter; worship; idolatry. (Gen 22:9-14; Ex 30:1-10; Rev 8:3; Gen 8:20; Ex 20:24-26; 2 Kings 11:18.)

Amber: God's presence or glory. (Ezek 1:4; Ezek 8:2.)

Ambulance: Help; rescue.

Amethyst: One of twelve stones found in high priest breastplate and in the foundation of the heavenly Jerusalem. (Ex 28:19; Rev 21:20.)

Anchor: Security; hope; safety. (Heb 6:18-19.)

Angel: God's help, provision or protection; messenger. (Gen 19:1; Dan 10:4-6; Luke 2:9-12; Rev 1:20.)

Ant: Hardworking; wise; nuisance. (Prov 6:6-8; Prov 30:24-25.)

Antenna: Necessary for clear transmission of messages; a need to pay close attention or tune in to the voice of God.

Antique: Things from the past; memories; generational issues inherited from ancestors (whether good or evil). (Jer 6:16.)

Apple: Wisdom; appreciation; fruit of the Spirit; refreshing; sin; temptation. (Ps 17:8; Prov 25:11; Gen 3:6; Matt 12:33-34; Gal 5:22-23; Deut 32:10; Song 2:5.)

Apprentice: Learning a specialized field of work. (1 Kings 19:19-21.)

Architect: Heavenly wisdom. (Prov 8:30; Heb 11:10.)

Archway: Opportunity; open heaven. (Ezek 40; Rev 4:1.)

Ark (ship): Divine promise; protection. (Gen 6:14; Ex 2:3.)

Ark of the testimony: The throne of God; covenant between man and God; humanity and deity in Christ; mediator. (Ex 25; Ex 26:34; Ex 40; Lev 16:2; Num 7:89; Heb 9; Heb 12:24.)

Arm: Strength or weakness: Savior; deliverer; reaching out to help; showing mercy; weapon. (Isa 53:1; Ps 136:12; Jer 17:5.)

Armor: Equipment for spiritual warfare. (Rom 13:12; Eph 6:10-18.)

Army: Angels of heaven; spiritual power; strength (whether good or evil). (Zech 6:1-8; Josh 5:13-14; 2 Sam 17:8-10; Rev 19:14-19; Rev 9:1-13.)

Arrow: Swiftness; deliverance; accusation; deceit; Satanic attack; judgment. (Ps 18:14; Jer. 9:8; Job 6:4; 2 Kings 13:17; Eph 6:16.)

Artist: Skill; talent; beauty; creative power; God. (Song 7:1; Isa 64:8.)

Ascend: To rise spiritually; intimacy with God; promotion; authority; progress; pride; self-righteousness. (Gen 11:4; Gen 28:12; 2 Kings 2:1; Isa 14:3; Amos 9:2; Ps 24:3; Mark 16:19; Eph 2:6; Rev 4:1.)

Ashes: Humility; repentance; poverty; mourning; sorrow; foolishness; plague; destruction; desolation. (Gen 18:27; Ex 9:8-10; 2 Sam 13:19; 1 Kings 13:3; Isa 58:5; Mal 4:3; Matt 11:21; Job 13:12; Ps 113:7.)

Assassin: Demon assigned to kill, steal, or destroy. (John 10:10.)

Asteroid: Divine message; destruction. (Rev 8:10.)

Astronaut: One who visits heavenly places; angel of God; fallen angel.

Athlete: One who is in spiritual training. (1 Cor 9:26; 1 Tim 4:8.)

Attic: The mind; memories; the subconscious.

Attorney: Skilled orator; representative of the law; our defender (Jesus); religious legalism. (Luke 5:17; Luke 10:25; 1 John 2:1; 1 Tim 1:7.)

Audit: Test; inspect; consider; weighed in the balance; judged. (Deut 13:3; Dan 3:16-18; Matt 19:3-12; James 1:3; James 1:12; 1 Cor 3:13.)

Aunt: Literal aunt; mature female Christian.

Author: Originator; designer; creator; Jesus; God the Father. (Heb 12:2; Job 19:23; Gen 1:1.)

Automobile: Life; an individual; ministry; church; business.

Autumn: Completion; end; change; repentance. (Isa 64:6; Jer 8:20; Jude 1:12.)

Awl: Used to pierce the ear of a devoted servant. (Ex 21:1-6.)

Axe: The word of God; rebuke; warning; repentance; arrogance; weakness; judgment. (Dan 4:14; Matt 3:7-12; Eccl 10:10; Isa 10:15.)

⋯ B ⋯

Baby: A new beginning; new idea; fulfillment of a promise; spiritual immaturity; dependent on others; helpless; innocence. (Acts 7:5; Rev 12:2-4; 1 John 2:12-14; Heb 5:12-13; Gal 4:4-6; 1 Cor 3:1.)

Babylon: Abundance and blessing; captivity; idolatry and rebellion; the object of God's judgment. (Isa 13:1-22; Rev 16:19; Rev 18:2-3.)

Back (body part): The past; unseen; secret; ignoring someone; resisting; burden; defeat. (Josh 7:12; Judg 20:42; 2 Chron 29:6; Phil 3:13; Matt 23:4.)

Back door: Past; secret; forgotten; unbelief; desertion; unfaithfulness; undercover; stealth; secret sin. (Gen 18:10; Gen 31:27; Matt 1:19; John 10:1.)

Bag: For carrying money or valuable items; spiritual gift; carrying a burden; compassion; faith; revelation; anger; resentment; a bag with holes is a symbol of financial or spiritual poverty. (Deut 25:13; Job 14:17; Matt 6:21; Mark 12:41-42; 2 Kings 5:23; Hag 1:6.)

Bait: Temptation; trap; entice; sin. (Job 41:1; 1 Cor 10:13.)

Bake: To prepare; to scheme.

Balance (scale): Honesty; fairness; integrity; business; considered; judgment. (Prov 11:1; Prov 16:11; Dan 5:27; Job 31:6.)

Bald: Humility; weakness; cleanness; judgment. (Jer 47:4-5; Jer 48:37; Ezek 7:18; Lev 13:40-44; Isa 3:24.)

Balm: Healing. (Jer 8:22; Jer 46:11; Jer 51:8.)

Bank: The heart; treasure; wealth; security; wisdom; heavenly resources; storehouse. (Luke 6:45; Luke 19:23; Matt 6:20; Col 2:2-3; Heb 11:26.)

Banner: Divine protection; warning; exalted; victory. (Ps 20:5; Song 2:4; Isa 13:2.)

Banquet: Intimate fellowship; celebration; abundance; divine favor; over-indulgence; lewdness. (Ps 23:5; Song 2:4; Est 5:4-6; Job 41:6; 1 Pet 4-3.)

Baptism: Death and resurrection; to bury one's old ways and be raised in the newness of eternal life. (Rom 6:1-11; Col 2:12-13.)

Barley: Inferiority; poverty; harvest. (Lev 27:16; Ruth 1:22; Num 5:15; Judg 7:13.)

Barn: Church; storehouse; wealth; greed; harvest; judgment. (Mal 3:10; Job 39:12; 2 Chron 32:28; Luke 12:18; Joel 1:17.)

Basket: The heart; first fruits; divine protection; provision; judgment. (Gen 40:16-17; Ex 2:3; Jer 24:1-10; Matt 16:9; Acts 9:25.)

Bat: Evil spirit; those who love darkness. (Isa 2:19-21.)

Bathing: Cleansing; sanctification; repentance; temptation. (Ps 51:2-3; Eph 5:25-26; 2 Sam 11:2.)

Bathroom: Condition of the heart; cleansing; purification; refreshing; renewal. (Eph 5:26; Isa 1:16.)

Battery: Reservoir of spiritual power; source of life; the Holy Spirit. (Luke 1:35; Luke 9:1; Acts 1:8.)

Battle: Spiritual warfare; conflict; disagreement. (Ps 144:1; Eph 6:10-12.)

Beach: Boundary between the earth and sea; separation between the physical and the spiritual; recreation; the location of ministry; a poor foundation; folly. (Prov 8:29; Job 38:11; Matt 7:26-27; Matt 13:48; John 21:4; Acts 21:5; Rev 10:2.)

Bear: Powerful adversary; oppressive leader or nation; financial matters (bear market). (2 Sam 17:8; Dan 7:5; Amos 5:19; 2 Kings 2:23-24; Prov 17:12.)

Beard: Manhood; spiritual maturity; holiness; God's judgment. (Lev 21:5; Ezek 5:1-6; 1 Chron 19:5.)

Beast: Kingdoms; principalities and powers; antichrist. (Dan 7:17-23; Rev 13:11-18.)

Beaver: Builder; industrious; ingenious; solitary.

Beaver: Industrious; busy; diligent; clever.

Bed: Rest; salvation; meditation; intimacy; peace; covenant (marriage); evil covenant (natural or spiritual adultery); sickness; suffering; death. (Ps 4:4; Ps 41:3; Isa 28:18-20; Eccl 4:11; Heb 13:4; Rev 2:22.)

Bees: Group of people; enemies who swarm; busy bodies; gossipers; may produce honey, or sting and wound. (1 Tim 5:13; Judg 14:8; Deut 1:44; Ps 118:12.)

Bell: Signal; God's presence; holiness; vanity; pride. (Ex 28:34; 1 Cor 13:1; Isa 3:16; Zech 14:20.)

Belly: The spirit or heart; emotions; selfishness; sickness; lust. (John 7:38; Prov 26:22; Phil 3:19.)

Belt: Truth; the word of God; strength; prophetic revelation; prophet. (Eph 6:14; Acts 21:11; 2 Kings 1:8; Isa 11:5; Isa 22:21; Matt 3:4.)

Bestiality: Works of darkness; a reprobate mind; idolatry; lust. (Lev 18:23; Rom 1:24-25.)

Bicycle: Humility; the power of the flesh as opposed to the power of the Spirit; self-righteousness. (Zech 4:6.)

Bikini: Transparency; uncovered or exposed; poverty; temptation; seduction. (2 Chron 28:15; Isa 47:3.)

Binoculars: Spiritual foresight, insight or oversight; heavenly perspective; supernatural understanding; prophetic vision; viewing a distant event;

fear of getting too close. (Gen 8:13; Gen 22:13; Gen 24:63; 1 Kings 18:43; Ezek 1:4; Ezek 10:1; Dan 12:5; Matt 4:1-10; 2 Cor 3:13.)

Bird: The believer; angels; the church; the Holy Spirit; God's provision; evil spirits; wicked rulers; a curse. (1 Kings 17:4-6; Matt 3:16; Matt 6:26; Matt 13:3-19; Prov 30:17; Song 5:11; Jer 12:9; Lam 4:19.)

Black: Without light or life; lacking the Spirit; poverty; famine; sickness; mourning; sin; evil; judgment; death. (Matt 6:23; 1 John 1:5; Jude 1:6; Jude 1:13; 2 Peter 2:17; Rev 6:5-6.)

Blanket: A covering for sin; authority. (Gen 9:23; 1 Kings 19:13; 2 Kings 2:14.)

Bleeding: Physical or emotional trauma; loss of spiritual life; sacrifice; circumcision; atonement; uncleanness; suffering; martyrdom; death. (Gen 4:10; Ex 4:25; Lev 15:19; Ps 147:3; Luke 22:44; Matt 27:35.)

Blindness: Spiritual or physical blindness; foolishness; dishonesty; self-righteousness; cursed; hatred. (Gen 19:11; Ex 23:8; Isa 56:10; Matt 15:14; Rom 11:25; Matt 23:26; 2 Pet 1:9; 1 John 2:11; Rev 3:17.)

Blister: Friction; disagreement; unforgiveness.

Blood: Life; spirit; covenant; atonement; redemption; testimony; witness; defiled; unclean; guilt; murder. (Gen 4:10; Ex 4:25; Lev 15:19; Lev 17:11; Ps 147:3; Luke 22:44; Matt 27:35; Ezek 33:8.)

Blood transfusion: Spiritual regeneration; salvation; deliverance. (Matt 26:28; 2 Cor 3:6.)

Blue: The heavens; the Holy Spirit; royalty; sadness. (Ex 24:10; Ezek 10:1; Ezek 1:26; Est 8:15.)

Blue: The Holy Spirit; priestly service; heaven; revelation; sadness (the blues). (Ex 26; Ex 39:22; Num 4:7-11.)

Boat: Church; life; person; ministry; supernatural transportation. (Matt 4:21; Matt 8:23; Mark 4:1; Mark 6:47-52; John 6:21; Acts 27.)

Boils: Curse; plague; testing. (Ex 9:8-10; Deut 28:7; Job 2:7.)

Bomb: Release of power; outpouring of the Spirit of God; sudden destruction; unexpected announcement; unresolved issue waiting to escalate (time bomb); explosive outburst. (Job 4:9; Acts 1:8.)

Bones: Support structure for the body; source of strength; contains physical or spiritual DNA; pertaining to genealogy or ancestry; condition of the heart; physical or spiritual death; (Gen 2:23; 1 Kings 13:31; Job 20:11; Job 30:17; Job 30:30; Job 40:18; Prov 16:24; Prov 17:22; Isa 58:11; Isa 66:14; Ezek 37; Hab 3;16; Matt 23:27.)

Book: Literal book; Bible; genealogy; memorial; covenant; record of salvation; record of divine revelation; human destiny; human wisdom; law; religious legalism; curse. (Gen 5:1; Deut 17:18; Ex 17:14; Ex 24:7; Ex 32-33; Num 5:23; Isa 29:11; Dan 7:10; Ezek 3; John 21:25; Rev 1:11; Rev 3:5; Rev 10:8-10; Rev 20:12.)

Boomerang: A good or evil deed repaid; sowing and reaping. (Isa 55:11; Prov 22:8; Hos 8:7; 2 Cor 9:6.)

Bottle: The heart; a vessel of the Holy Spirit; wineskin. (Job 32:19; Matt 9:17.)

Bow (see arrow)

Box: Treasure; the soul; confined; spiritual gift. (John 12:6; Rom 1:11.)

Bra: Support; integrity and uprightness; confine.

Bracelet: Betrothal; pledge; offering. (Gen 24:22; Gen 24:47; Num 31:50; Isa 3:19; 2 Kings 13:14-19.)

Braces (teeth): Restricted speech; religious legalism; lacking wisdom.

Brakes: Slow or stop; warning to proceed with caution or exercise discernment. (Ps 32:9; James 1:26; Gal 5:22-23.)

Branch: Jesus; the believer; peace (olive branch); hope; spiritual life; anointing; ancestry; abomination. (Gen 8:11; Jer 23:5; Zech 3:8; Isa 60:21; John 12:13; John 15:2-5; Isa 14:19.)

Brass: Judgment; strength; refined; idolatry; ungodly people; prideful. (Ex 27:2; Ex 30:18; Num 21:9; Jer 6:28; Ezek 22:18; 1 Cor 13:1; Rev 1:15.)

Bread: Sustaining life; the word of God; Christ; God's presence; communion; the church; provision; sin (unleavened). (Ezek 4:9-17; 1 Sam 21:6; Lev 24:5–7; 1 Cor 5:8; Matt 4:4; Judg 7:13-14; John 6:31-51.)

Breast: Source of nourishment; intimacy; abundance; beauty; repentance; idolatry; lewdness. (Gen 24:25; Job 3:12; Ps 22:9; Prov 5:19; Song 1:13; Ezek 23:21; Nah 2:7; John 21:20.)

Breastplate: Righteousness; judgment; covering or protection for the heart; defense. (Ex 28:15-30; Eph 6:14.)

Breath: The Holy Spirit; God's power; life; offense. (Gen 2:7; Gen 6:17; Job 4:9; Job 19:17; Job 32:8; Job 33:4; John 20:22; Rev 3:15.)

Brick: Slavery; work of man; idolatry; imitation stone. (Gen 11:3; Ex 1:14; Isa 65:3.)

Bride: The object of God's affection; Israel; the church; the Christian; heavenly Jerusalem; martyr. (Isa 62:5; Jer 2:32; Hos 4:13; Matt 9:15; John 3:29; Rev 21:2; Rev 22:17.)

Bridge: Place of transition or trial; way of escape; to join; the cross; Christ; divine path; passage between life and death or heaven and earth. (2 Kings 2:8; Gen 28:12; Gen 32:22; Num 32:29; Deut 11:31; Josh 3:6-17; Matt 7:13-14; 1 Corinthians 10:13.)

Bridle: Control; restraint. (Ps 32:9; James 1:26.)

Broom: Cleaning; deliverance; setting things in order; searching. (Dan 11:26; Isa 14:23; Luke 11:25; Luke 15:8; John 2:15.)

Brother-in-law: Natural brother-in-law; legalistic Christian; adversary. (Luke 5:17; 1 Tim 1:5-7; Col 2:16.)

Brother: Natural brother; a fellow believer; Jesus; one who is like-minded; protector. (Gen 4:9; Prov 17:17; Prov 18:9; Prov 18:24; Matt 4:18; Matt 5:23; Matt 2:48-49; Matt 18:15; Col 4:7; Rev 1:9.)

Brown: Earthly; made of earth; humble; dead. (Gen 30:32-40; Isa 15:62; Cor 4:7.)

Bruise: Victory; tender spot; wound; spiritual attack; slander; sinful. (Gen 3:15; Job 5:18; Isa 1:6; Isa 42:3; Isa 53:5.)

Bubble: Spirit; angel; demon; protection; fragile; thought; enclosure. (Ezek 1:15-16; Ezek 1:22; Ezek 1:26-27; Job 1:10; Prov 18:10.)

Bubble gum: Childish; immature; to "chew" on a matter is to consider it. (Prov 22:15; 1 Cor 13:11; Dan 4:5; Job 37:14.)

Bud: New life. (Num 17:8; Isa 61:1.)

Building: Individual; institution; business; the church; heavenly mansion. (Ezek 41:15; Ezek 42; Mark 13:1-2; Luke 6:48; Rev 21:10.)

Bull: Strength; economic increase; offering; reckless; idol; pride; evil spirit. (Ex 29:11; Ps 22:12; Jer 31:18; Jer 50:11; Hos 12:11.)

Bullet: God's word; a harsh word; spiritual weapon (good or evil). (Deut 32:42; Ps 64:3; Jer 9:80.)

Burn: To consume; to purify; holy; passion; burden; wrath; judgment; destroy; torment; lust. (Ex 3:2-6; Job 1:16; Job 30:30; Ps 11:6; Ps 39:3; Jer 20:9; Matt 3:12; Rom 1:27; Rev 19:20.)

Bus: Church; large ministry; teaching ministry (school bus).

Bush: The presence of God; hiding place; unfruitfulness; humility. (Ex 3:2-4; Deut 33:16; Luke 6:44.)

Butter: The fruit of labor; wealth; deceptive words. (Gen 18:8; Ps 55:21; Prov 30:33; Isa 7:15.)

Butterfly: Transformation (from caterpillar to butterfly); new life; freedom; glorified body; fragile; flighty. (2 Cor 3:18; 2 Cor 5:17; Rom 12:2; Eph 4:14.)

··· **C** ···

Cage: Imprisonment; restriction; stronghold. (Ezek 19:9; Jer 37:15; Rev 18:2.)

Cake: Divine food; man's provision; sin. (Gen18:6; 1 Kings 19:6; Jer 7:18; Hos 7:8.)

Calculator: Problem solving; counting the cost; considering in totality. (Job 28:25-26; Luke 9:62; Luke 14:28.)

Calendar: Divine timing; planning; appointment. (Dan 9:2-2; Dan 2:21; Matt 16:3; Acts 1:7.)

Camel: Servant's heart; burden bearing; a treasured possession; endurance. (Gen 24:11; Isa 30:6; Jer 49:32.)

Camera: Self-image; public image; publicity; fame; record; spiritual vision; memories; memorial; the soul. (1 Cor 13:12; Acts 3:4; Ex 13:9.)

Cancer: Literal cancer; self-destructive thoughts; bitterness; shame; envy; fear. (Prov 12:4; Prov 14:30; Hab 3:16.)

Candle: Spiritual light; the Holy Spirit; the church; the word of God; wisdom; the eye. (Ex 25; 2 Sam 22:29; Job 12:5; Job 21:17; Ps 119:105; Prov 6:23; Prov 20:27; Matt 5:15; Matt 6:22 Matt 25:1-8; Rev 1:12-20; Rev 4:5.)

Cards: Battle; taking risk; strategy; transparency (put your cards on the table); self-deception; divination (tarot); underhanded dealing; wisdom (knowing when to fold). (Jonah 1:7; Acts 1:26; Luke 14:31.)

Carnival: Pleasure; entertainment; allure; carnality; carelessness. (Job 1:13; Isa 22:13; Matt 24:38; Luke 21:34.)

Carpenter: Builder; spiritual leader; Christ. (Matt 13:55.)

Castle: Fortress; stronghold; sanctuary; person; ministry; heavenly home; church; kingdom; habitation of evil spirits; dungeon. (Jer 6:27; Ps 18:2; Ps 91:2; Ps 144:2.)

Cat: Valued friend; curiosity; self-willed; stealth; unteachable; evil spirit; witchcraft. (Ezek 19:3; Jer 5:6; 13: 23; Hos 13:7.)

Caterpillar: Unredeemed; judgment; plague; destructive power. (Joel 1:4; Isa 33:4; Ps 78:46.)

Cave: Seclusion; shelter; stronghold; hiding place; inner world of the soul; secret place; reclusive; tomb. (Gen 19:30; Gen 25:9; Josh 10:16; 1 Kings 18:4; 1 Kings 19:9; 1 Chron 11:15; John 11:38.)

Censer: Literal incense burner; prayer; intercession; worship. (Lev 16:12; Rev 8:3.)

Chain: Captivity; slavery; imprisonment; oppression; joining together; wealth. (Acts 12:6; Isa 40:19; Prov 1:9.)

Chair: Authority; rest; judgment. (1 Kings 22:10; Ruth 3:18; Matt 27:19.)

Cheek: Unconditional love; beauty; persecution; reproach; sorrow. (1 Kings 22:24; Job 16:10; Ps 3:7; Song 1:10; Lam 1:2; Matt 5:39.)

Chest: Love; the heart; righteousness; judgment. (John 13:23; Eph 6:14; Ex 28:29.)

Chew: Metaphorically, to meditate on or consider a matter.

Chicken: God; a pastor; one who gathers; one who is fearful. (Isa 49:5; Matt 23:37.)

Chicks: Offspring; one's disciples; children of God. (Isa 49:5; Matt 23:37.)

Children: Children of God; one's inner child; innocence; inheritance; childishness; ignorance; children of the devil. (Rom 8:14; Ps 17:14; Matt 11:25; 1 Cor 3:1; Acts 13:10.)

Church (building): A particular church congregation or denomination; the church in general; the believer; a place of worship. (Matt 16:18; Eph 5:23-29; Col 1:18; Rev 1:11.)

Circle: God; the earth; the sea; the heavens; without beginning or end; completion; repetition. (Job 22:14; Prov 8:27; Isa 40:22; Mark 3:34; Ps 19:6.)

City: A place of security (city of refuge); a place of authority; heavenly Jerusalem; worldliness. (Gen 13:12; Num 35:6; Luke 19:7.)

Clay: The weakness of mankind; frailty; earthly. (Job 10:9; Isa 64:8; Dan 2:33)

Clock: Times and seasons; strategic timing; revelation of the timing of an event; divinely ordained time; waiting on God's timing; appointment; opportunity; watchfulness. (Dan 9:2; Dan 9:24-27; Matt 24:36; 1 John 2:18; Acts 1:7.)

Closet: Private matters; a place of prayer; secret sin. (Matt 6:6; Luke 12:2-3.)

Clothing: Righteousness; salvation; God's glory; man-made covering for sin; condition of the heart. (Gen 3:7; Job 29:14; Dan 12:7; Rom 13:14; James 2:2; Isa 64:6.)

Cloud: God's glory; God's presence; God's promise; God's favor; concealment; covering; revival. (Gen 9:13; Ex 13:21; Ex 40:34-38; Prov 16:15.)

Clown: Entertainer; attention seeker; people pleaser; fool. (Eccl 2:1-3; Ps 49:10 Prov 14:8; Prov 14:29.)

Coat (cloak, mantle, robe): One's occupation; righteousness; spiritual authority; God's anointing; protection; grief; shame; self-righteousness; religious legalism. (Gen 37:3; Lev 8:7; 1 Kings 19:13-19; Matt 3:4; Luke 20:46; John 19:5; Rev 4:4.)

Coffee: Stimulant; wake-up call; to become sober. (Rom 13:11; Eph 5:14; 1 Pet 5:8.)

Coin: Wealth; divine provision; reward; something of value; payment; bribe. (Gen 20:16; Zech 11:12; Ps 119:72; Matt 10:29; Luke 15:8; Matt 26:15.)

Compass: Direction; position; bearing. (Rev 7:1; Rev 20:8.)

Computer: Means of communication; something that is programmed; a programmed way of thinking or operating.

Concrete: The devices of man; foundation; solid; durable; inflexible; hard-hearted; set in one's ways. (Gen 11:31 Kings 6:37; Ex 4:21; Nah 3:14.)

Cord: Life; redemption; link; bloodline or genealogy; used to bind or bring together; control or manipulate; sin; bondage. (Gen 38:28; Prov 5:22; Eccl 4:12; Eccl 12:6; Acts 9:25.)

Corn: God's word; the believer; harvest; increase; blessing. (Gen 41:5; Isa 55:10-11; Matt 13; John 12:24; 1 Cor 15:36.)

Cornerstone: Christ; foundation. (Ps 118:22; Isa 28:16; Matt 21:42.)

Court: God's government; justice; redemption; legalism; judgment. (Deut 25:1; Ps 100:4; Dan 7:10; Zech 3:7.)

Cow: One of the four faces of God; sacrifice; wealth; idol. (Lev 22:19; Ex 32; Ezek 1:10; Ps 50:10.)

Crimson: Blood; redemption; sin; suffering; sacrifice. (Isa 1:8; Jer 4:30.)

Crocodile: See alligator.

Cross: The cross Jesus died on; salvation from sin; reconciliation to God; healing; sacrifice; sin; a curse; death. (Matt 10:38; Matt 27:32; 1 Cor 1:18; Eph 2:16; Heb 12:2.)

Crossroad: Making a decision; change. (Gen 13:9-11; Acts 15:37-39.)

Crow: God's minister of justice or provision; the believer; unclean spirit; (Gen 8:7; 1 Kings 17:4; Prov 30:17; Luke 12:24.)

Crown: Authority; rulership; honor; reward; eternal life. (2 Kings 11:12; 1 Pet 5:4; James 1:12; 1 Thess 2:19; Rev 6:2.)

Crystal ball: Vision; the future; divination; fortune telling; witchcraft. (Deut 18:10; 2 Kings 21:6; Acts 19:19.)

Cup: Wealth; provision; life; death; sacrifice; righteousness; communion; instrument of punishment or judgment. (Gen 40:11; Gen 44:2; Ps 11:6; Ps 23:5; Isa 51:17; Matt 20:22; Matt 23:25; Matt 26:39; John 18:11; 1 Cor 10:16.)

Curtain: Veil; a device that conceals; covering; separation between God and man. (Ex 26:33; Matt 27:51; 2 Cor 3:14.)

Cymbal: Praise; worship; noise; pride; foolishness. (Ps 150:5; 1 Cor 13:1.)

··· **D** ···

Dam: Potential; stored power; blockage; resistance to the flow of the Holy Spirit.

Dancing: Worship; joy; romance; seduction; lewdness; idolatry. (Ex 32:19; Ps 30:11; Job 21:7-13; 1 Sam 18:6; Mark 6:22; 1 Cor 10:7.)

Darkness: Spiritual blindness; ignorance; sorrow; wickedness; death. (Isa 9:2; Job 10:21; John 8:12; Rom 1:21; 1 Thess 5:5.)

Dart: Swiftness; deliverance; accusation; deceit; Satanic attack; judgment. (Ps 18:14; Jer. 9:8; Job 6:4; 2 Kings 13:17; Eph 6:16.)

Daughter: Natural daughter; descendant; spiritual daughter, e.g., a student, disciple, or protege; new believer; the dreamer at a young age; a child of God. (Luke 13:16; Mark 5:34; Matt 12:46-50; Rom 8:16-17; 1 Tim 5:2; Titus 2:2-5.)

Daylight: Godliness; knowledge; truth; goodness. (Gen 1:4; 1 Cor 3:13; 2 Cor 4:6; Eph 5:13; 1 Thess 5:5.)

Deafness: Physical deafness; stubbornness; indifference; spiritual ignorance. (Mic 7:16; Isa 42:18.)

Death: Literal death; transformation from spiritual death to life; separation; the end of a relationship or ministry; change; sin. (Job 3:5; Job 28:22; Rom 8:13; Heb 2:14; 1 John 3:14; 1 John 5:16; James 1:15.)

Debt: Sin; unforgiveness; responsibility. (Deut 15; Matt 6:12; Rom 8:12.)

Deed: God's blessing; inheritance; ownership; contract. (Gen 23:14-18; Heb 9:15; Heb 9:15-16; Heb 11:8.)

Deer: Attentive to the things of God; loving; swift; agile; graceful; sure-footed; timid. (2 Sam 22:34; Isa 35:6; Prov 5:19.)

Dentist: Since teeth often speak of wisdom, a dentist may represent the Lord, who gives wisdom.

Desert: A place of trial, testing, humbling, or chastening; a place of dependence on God; a place of solitude; infertility; a lack of intimacy with God. (Num 32:13; Deut 2:7; Ps 102:6; Isa 35:1-6; Luke 4:1-2.)

Dew: God's favor, provision or gift; revelation, guidance, or confirmation from God; the Holy Spirit. (Gen 27:28; Num 11:9; Hos 14:5; Judg 6:37-40; Ps 133:3.)

Diamond: Precious; enduring; permanent; hard-hearted. (Jer 17:1; Ezek 3:9; Ezek 28:13; Prov 17:8; 1 Pet 2:4.)

Diary: One's thoughts and intentions; secret desires; the human heart; book of remembrance; testimony; record; memories. (Ex 17:14; Jer 30:2; John 21:25; Luke 1:1-3.)

Dining room: A place of fellowship; communion; spiritual nourishment. (Ps 23:5; John 13:18-30; Rev 19:9.)

Dirt: Humanity; weakness; frailty; sin; death. (Gen 2:7; Job 4:19; Job 7:21; 1 Cor 15:49.)

Disease: Physical sickness; spiritual weakness or vulnerability; sin. (Ex 23:25; Eccl 5:17; Prov 14:30.)

Ditch: Passion; habit; religious tradition; addiction; lust; sin. (Deut 28:14; Matt 15:14; Psalm 7:15; Prov 23:27.)

Divorce: Literal divorce; spiritual separation; physical separation; parting of ways; adultery; idolatry; unfaithfulness. (Isa 50:1; Jer 3:1; Mal 2:16; Hos 2; 2 Cor 6:14.)

Doctor: Literal physician; Christ; spiritual authority; healing ministry; counselor. (Job 13:4; Jer 8:22; Matt 9:12.)

Dog: Loyal friend; watchdog; guardian; unbeliever; mocker; evil spirit; enemy. (Ps 22:16; Isa 56:10-11; Matt 7:6; Matt 15:27; Phil 3:2; Rev 22:15.)

Donkey: Lowly or humble; obedient servant; self-willed; single-minded; obstinate. (Prov 26:3; Isa 1:3; Jer 22:19; Hos 8:9; Zech 9:9; Matt 21:7.)

Door: Christ; access to God; entrance; protection; opportunity; decision; escape; temptation; barrier; change; the mouth. (Gen 4:7; Ex 12:23; Job 3:10; Job 31:9; Job 38:8-10; Job 41:14; Ps 24:7-9; John 10:7; Col 4:3; Ps 141:3.)

Dove: The Holy Spirit; peace; new life; innocence; offering to God. (Gen 8:8-12; Matt 3:16; Lev 5:7.)

Dragon: Satan; demon; antichrist; wickedness. (Rev 12:3-9; Rev 13:2-4; Rev 16:13-14.)

Drink: Communion with God; to accept; to be satisfied; celebrate; joy; revival; refreshing; sacrifice; to receive punishment or judgment; drunkenness; sin. (Gen 19:32; Gen 35:14; Job 6:4; Job 34:7; Ps 36:8; Ps 75:8; Prov 4:17; Prov 20:1; Eccl 2:24; Eccl 9:7; Isa 66:11; Matt 20:22; Matt 26:42; 1 Cor 10:4; 1 Cor 10:21; Rev 14:8-10.)

Drown: To be overwhelmed; in need of salvation; grief; sorrow; temptation; excessive debt; judgment. (1 Tim 6:9; Isa 61:3; Jonah 2:3; Jer 47:2.)

Drugs: Medicine; a health problem; divine healing; under the influence of a spell; sorcery; witchcraft; addiction; control; rebellion; deception; religious legalism; sin. (Jer 8:22; Jer 30:13; Prov 17:22; Rev 9:21 (pharmakeia) Gal 3:1.)

Drum: Instrument of praise; weapon of spiritual warfare. (Ex 15:20; Ps 81:2; Ps 150:4-6; Ezek 28:13.)

Dust storm: Literal windstorm; sudden and unexpected change; dramatic work of God; the Holy Spirit; the voice of God; the glory of God; judgment; destruction; (2 Kings 2:11; Job 38:1; Ps 58:9 Ps 77:18; Prov 1:27; Prov 10:25; Jer 23:19; Ezek 1:4; Hos 8:7; Nah 1:3.)

Dynamite: Power of the Holy Spirit; destruction. (Luke 9:1; Acts 1:8; Rev 18:9-10.)

··· E ···

Eagle: One of the four faces of God; the Holy Spirit; Israel; prophet; angel; human spirit; protector; strength; swiftness. (Ezek 1:10; Isa 40:31; Ex 19:4; Job 9:26; Rev 12:14.)

Earthquake: The power of God; upheaval; change; crisis; disaster; judgment. (Matt 27:54; Matt 28:2; Acts 16:26; Isa 29:6; Heb 12:26-27; Jer 4:24; Rev 11:13.)

East: God's glory; beginning; newness; eastern culture or traditions. (Gen 2:8; Job 1:3; Isa 2:6; Ezek 11:23; Ps 103:12; Matt 2:1.)

Eat: To receive physical or spiritual nourishment; to receive revelation from God; to commune with others; to partake; to agree with or accept. (Isa 55:1; Ezek 3:1; Mark 2:16; Matt 26:26; Acts 10:12-15; Rev 3:20; Rev 10:10.)

Egg: Natural or spiritual DNA; God's promise or gift; a new idea or plan; new beginning; hope; potential; revelation; fragile. (Luke 11:12-13; Luke 24:49; Ezek 17:51; Luke 17:6.)

Eight: New beginning; physical or spiritual circumcision (regeneration); eternity. (Gen 21:4; Num 29:35; Matt 28:1; John 20:19; 1 Pet 3:20.)

Electricity: The power of the Holy Spirit; healing; danger. (Luke 9:1; Acts 1:8; Acts 5:5; 1 Cor 2:4.)

Elephant: Powerful minister; popular ministry; thick-skinned; not easily offended; one who has a good memory.

Elevator (escalator): Change of position in life: moving in the spiritual realm; natural or spiritual promotion or demotion. (Obad 1:4; Rev 4:1; Ps 75:6-7; Prov 3:35; Luke 10:18.)

Eleven: Incomplete. (Gen 32:22 and Gen 37:9 compared with Gen 49:28; Matt 28:16; Acts 1:26.)

Engine: Source of power; human heart; human spirit; (Ps 7:9; Prov 20:27; Jer 17:10; Rom 8:27.)

Envelope (see letter)

Evening: Fading glory; time when Christ is not physically present on the earth; a time when the works of darkness are done; the end of life. (Gen 29:23; Ps 59:6; Prov 7:9-13; Rom 13:12; 1 Thess 5:5-7; Rev 22:5.)

Evergreen: Long life; health; prosperity; majesty; man; Ps 92:12 Song 5:15; Isa 14:8; Dan 4:20-22.)

Eye: Physical or spiritual perception; God's omniscience or omnipresence; knowledge; insight; foresight; oversight; desire (whether good or evil); passion; lust; window to the soul. (Eccl 2:10; Eccl 2:14; Prov 23:5; Prov 27:20; Ps 101:3; Job 16:20; Luke 11:34; Eph 1:18; Rev 3:18.)

··· F ···

Face: Personhood; identity; character; countenance; pertaining to an object or person's physical appearance. (Gen 1:2; Prov 7:15; Prov 16:15; Prov 21:29; Prov 27:19; Jer 1:8; Job 16:8; Matt 6:16; Luke 9:51.)

Falling: Reverence or worship; change of position; the result of being lifted up with pride; demotion; loss of control; correction; disfavor; trapped; apostasy; judgment; death. (Rev 7:11; Judg 13:20; Rev 17:10; Rev 18:2; Luke 10:18; Prov 16:18; Ps 7:15; 2 Thess 2:3.)

Family: Natural or spiritual family; the family of God; the church; those with similar views and beliefs (whether good or bad); one's circle of friends. (Matt 12:48-50; John 8:44; Eph 2:19.)

Famine: Natural or spiritual starvation or poverty; judgment. (Amos 8:11; Ps 37:19; 2 Kings 6:25; Acts 11:28; Rev 18:18.)

Farm: The kingdom of God; the church; the ministry of the believer; Israel. (Gen 9:20; Isa 61:5; Matt 21:33-46; 2 Tim 2:6.)

Father-in law: Natural father-in-law; spiritual mentor; leader; a relationship based on legalism. (Ex 3:1; 1 Sam 4:21; 1 Sam 18:18; Matt 10:35.)

Father: One's natural father or ancestor; God the Father; Christ; spiritual authority such as a pastor; caretaker; Satan, the father of lies. (Gen 22:7; Job 17:14; Job 29:16; Isa 9:6; Isa 51:2; Isa 64:8; Matt 3:9; Matt 5:16; John 5:18; Matt 23:9.)

Feathers: Divine protection; Holy Spirit; angels. (Ps 61:4; Ps 91:4; Isa 6:2; Rev 4:8.)

Feet: The condition of one's natural feet; one's spiritual "walk," or how one navigates the path of life; the ministry of a messenger; stubborn or steadfast (unmoving); rebellion (kicking); feet that run to commit sin. (Job 18:8; Matt 18:8; Prov 19:2; Ps 8:6; Ps 18:33; Ps 31:8; Ps 58:10; Ps 66:9; Ps 119:105.)

Fence: Protection or fortification; boundary; limitation; device used to control people; source of division; offense ("a fence"); imprisonment. (Deut 3:5; Jer 1:15; Num 32:17; John 10:1-9.)

Field: Wealth; the world; the church; Israel; the believer; the heart. (Ruth 2:2-9; Ps 103:15; Prov 24:30-34; Isa 32:16; Matt 13:3-44; Matt 20:1-16; Matt 21:33-46.)

Fifteen: God's grace. (2 Kings 20:6; Hos 3:2.)

Fifty: Jubilee; liberty; Pentecost. (Lev 25:8-10; Luke 16:6.)

Fig: The nation of Israel; prosperity; self-righteousness (fig leaves); religious legalism. (Gen 3:7; Prov 27:18; Isa 34:4; Isa 36:16; Hos 2:12; Hos 9:10; Luke 13:6-9; Matt 24:32-35.)

Fingerprint: Identity; ownership; source; evidence; genealogy. (Ex 8:19; Ex 31:18; Luke 11:20.)

Fire: God's presence; God's glory; the angelic; life; passion; zeal; purification; testing; consuming; sickness; judgment; eternal torment. (Gen 19:24; Ex 3:2; Ex 9:23-24; Ex 24:17; 1 Kings 18:38; 2 Kings 2:11; Job 18:5; Ps 39:3; Ps 57:4; Ps 79:5; Ps 104:4; Rev 3:18; Rev 8:5; Rev 20:10.)

Fish: Men's souls. (Eccl 9:12; Matt 4:19.)

Fish hook: Evangelism; temptation; being compelled against one's will. (Matt 4:19; 2 Chron 33:11; Job 41:1; Ezek 29:4; Matt 17:27.)

Five: Military tactics; stewardship; fivefold ministry. (Lev 26:8; 1 Sam 17:40; Isa 30:17; Isa 19:18; Matt; 25:2; Matt 25:15-20; Luke 19:18-19; Eph 4:11-12.)

Flag: Nationality; genealogy; God's presence; devotion to or worship of God; emblem; military insignia. (Ex 17:15; Ps 20:5; Ps 60:4; Ps 74:4; Song 2:4; Isa 11:10; Isa 30:17.)

Flies: Evil spirits; plague; judgment; (Ex 8:22; Ps 78:45; Eccl 10:1.)

Flood: Literal flood; God's increasing glory; revival; sudden change; overflow; overwhelm; testing; judgment. (Gen 6:17; Job 27:20; Ps 69:2; Song 8:7; Isa 44:3; Isa 59:19; Dan 9:26; Jonah 2:3; Jer 12:5; Matt 7:25-27; 1 Pet 4:4.)

Floor: Foundation; elementary principles; beginning; primary; humility; grounded. (Ps 11:31; Ps 97:2; Prov 8:29; 1 Cor 3:10-12; Eph 2:20; 1 Tim 6:19; Heb 6:1; Rev 21:14.)

Flower: The fading glory or fleeting existence of man; God's provision; innocence; virginity. (Isa 28:1; Job 14:2; Ps 103:15; Luke 12:27-28; 1 Cor 7:36; James 1:10-11.)

Flying: Moving in the spirit; rising above earthly matters; moving closer to God; taking shelter; flying high gives one a higher perspective; flying too high may symbolize pride; flying out of control may signal danger. (Ex 19:4; Isa 40:31; Isa 14:33; Zech 5:9; Jer 48:40; Ps 55:6; Rev 12:14.)

Fog: Concealment; spiritual or natural blindness; fleeting. (Hos 6:4; Hos 13:3; Acts 13:11; Isa 44:22; 2 Pet 2:17.)

Footprint (see fingerprint)

Forest: Wealth; protection; a nation; concealed danger or works of darkness; lost. (Num 13:20; 2 Kings 19:23; Ps 104:20; Isa 10:18; Isa 22:8; Jer 5:6; Ezek 15:6.)

Fortress: God; protection; stronghold; sanctuary. (Prov 18:10; Ps 18:2; Ps 31:2; Ps 144:2; Isa 34:13.)

Forty: Testing; trial. (Gen 7:4; Ex 24:18; Josh 5:6; Matt 4:2.)

Foundation: Elementary principles; Christ; beginning; primary; humility; grounded. (Ps 11:31; Ps 97:2; Prov 8:29; 1 Cor 3:10-12; Eph 2:20; 1 Tim 6:19; Heb 6:1; Rev 21:14.)

Fountain: The source of water; the Holy Spirit; the source of life; womb; the source of wisdom; the human spirit or heart; origin; abundance.

(Gen 7:11; Deut 33:28; Ps 36:9; Prov 5:18; Prov 13:14; Prov 14:27; Song 4:12; Jer 6:7; Rev 21:6.)

Four-wheel drive: Ministry that operates outside of well-worn paths and traditions; independent; unconfined; capable of traveling difficult roads and enduring persecution. (Matt 7:14; Acts 27:7-8; 2 Cor 11:23-28; Luke 1:80.)

Four: Rule or dominion, particularly over the earth; global in scope. (Dan 2:39-40; Dan 7:6; Dan 7:17; Dan 8:8; Dan 8:22; Dan 11:1-4; Rev 7:1-4.)

Fourteen: Passover. (Lev 23:5; 1 Kings 8:65.)

Fox: Sly, cunning or deceptive; cowardly; one who does evil silently or under the cover of night; evil spirit; seemingly insignificant sin. (Ezek 13:4; Luke 13:32; Song 2:15.)

Frog: Evil spirit; the judgment of God. (Ex 8:1-12; Ps 78:45; Rev 16:13.)

Front door: An entrance; the future; opportunity; transition; the mouth; the heart. (Gen 4:7; Job 31:9; Job 41:14; John 10:7.)

Fruit: The consequences of one's actions; the evidence of one's motives; the evidence of the work of the Holy Spirit; natural or spiritual offspring; increase; (Gen 9:1; Ps 1:3; Ps 104:13; Ps 127:3; Ps 132:11; Prov 11:30; Prov 18:21; Matt 7:15-17; Gal 5:22-23.)

Funeral: Literal funeral; burying one's past life; preparing for resurrection; baptism. (Matt 26:2; Rom 6:4-6; 1 Cor 15:12-20.)

··· **G** ···

Garage: Literal garage; natural or spiritual inactivity; a ministry under repair. (1 Sam 22:1; 1 Kings 19:9; Luke 1:80.)

Garbage: Rejected; judged; sin; religious works. (Jer 49:13; Isa 5:25; Isa 25:10; Ps 83:10; Phil 3:4-7.)

Garden: God's kingdom; the world; the human spirit or heart; the church; place of idol worship; sex organs. (Gen 2:8-18; Song 4:16; Song 5:1; Song 6:2-11; Isa 65:3; Luke 13:19.)

Gasoline: Fuel; a source of power; the Holy Spirit; prayer; strife, contention or anger. (Job 1:16; Job 4:9; Job 21:17; Prov 26:20-21; Ps 21:9; Rev 4:5.)

Gate: Christ; access to God; entrance; place of control or authority (gatekeeper); protection; barrier; opportunity; way of escape; (2 Sam 15:2; Ps 24:7-9; 2 Kings 7:10; John 10:1-10; Prov 1:21; Rev 21:21.)

General (military): Literal military leader; church leader; Christ; an angel. (Josh 5:13-15; 1 Sam 9:16; 1 Sam 13:14; 1 Cor 12:28; Eph 4:11-12.)

Giant: A strong enemy; spirit of fear; difficult test; an angel; great faith. (Gen 6:4; Num 13:33; Ps 27:12; 2 Sam 21:15-22; Matt 8:10; Matt 17:20; 1 Cor 16:9.)

Gift: A literal gift; gift of the Holy Spirit; God's provision; Christ; peace; salvation; sacrifice; talent; knowledge; anointing; (Ps 68:18; Prov 18:16; Eccl 5:19; Matt 2:11; Matt 7:11; John 4:10; John 14:27; 1 Cor 7:7; 1 Cor 12:1-31; Eph 2:8; James 1:17.)

Girl: Literal girl; immature female believer; future generation; innocence; full of faith; teachable; simple minded. (Ps 34:11; Ps 78:6; Matt 11:16; Matt 18:3; Matt 19:13-14; 1 Cor 14:20.)

Glass: Mirror; reflecting one's identity; motives of the heart revealed; provides an imperfect view; fragile. (Prov 27:19; 1 Cor 13:12; 2 Cor 3:18; James 1:23.)

Goat: Stubborn; self-willed; unbelieving; unredeemed; earthly kingdom. (Ezek 34:17; Dan 8:21; Matt 25:31-46.)

Gold: Divinity; material wealth; God's glory; spiritual life; kingship; beauty; wisdom; sacrifice; the believer's works; pride; idolatry. (Gen 13:2; Dan 2:38; Ex 20:23; Ex 25:11-18; Prov 3:14; Prov 25:11; Song 5:11-15; 1 Cor 3:12-13; Rev 1:13; Rev 4:4; Rev 14:14.)

Grandchild: Literal grandchild; spiritual offspring; future generation. (Gen 22:17; Deut 4:9; Ps 78:5-7; Joel 1:3.)

Grandparent: Literal grandparents or ancestors; spiritual or natural inheritance (whether good or evil); spiritual or natural traditions; God the Father. (Gen 17:4-5; Gen 31:53; Ex 20:5; Lev 26:40; Dan 7:9.)

Grapes: The consequences of one's action; fruit of the Spirit; blood sacrifice; object of wrath. (Gen 49:11; Isa 5:2-4; Jer 25:30; Matt 7:16; Gal 5:22-23; Rev 14:19-20.)

Grass: The frailty of humanity: godliness; numerous; withered; nourishment; refreshment. (2 Sam 23:3-4; Job 5:25; Ps 23:2; Ps 37:2; Ps 92:7; Ps 102:4; Ps 103:15; Matt 6:30; James 1:11.)

Grasshopper: Plague; judgment; numerous; small. (Num 13:33; 1 Kings 8:37; Jer 46:23.)

Grave: Rest; resurrection; concealment; darkness; despair; sin; death. (Job 7:9; Job 14:13; Ps 30:3; Ps 49:15; Matt 23:27; Matt 28:1-6.)

Gray hair: Elderly; spiritually mature; wise; deserving of honor; an attribute of God the Father; approaching death. (Dan 7:9; Gen 42:38; Prov 16:31; Rev 1:14.)

Green: Life; eternal life; prosperity; growth; envy; inexperience. (Gen 1:30; Job 15:32; Ps 23:2; Isa 15:6.)

Groom: God the Father; Christ; a married man. (Isa 61:10; Matt 9:15; Matt 25:5-6; Rev 18:23.)

Gun: Implement of warfare; hurtful or threatening words; accusation; spiritual weapon; (1 Sam 17:40; 1 Sam 21:8; 2 Sam 1:27; Job 20:24; Isa 54:17; 2 Cor 10:4.)

··· **H** ···

Hail: God's glory; judgment. (Ex 9:23; Ps 18:12-13; Hag 2:17; Rev 8:7.)

Hair: Covering; glory; strength; innumerable; protection; sanctification; prophetic ministry; vanity; dishonor. (2 Sam 14:25-26; Ps 40:12; Prov 16:31; Song 7:5; Isa 3:24; Zech 13:4; Matt 3:4; Acts 18:18; 1 Cor 11:14-15; Rev 1:14.)

Hallway: Path of life; path of opportunity; way of salvation; way of righteousness; making a choice; time of transition; passageway to the future or past. (Ps 1:1; Ps 17:5; Ps 23:3; Prov 2:8; Num 22:25-26; Ex 14:22; Jer 18:15.)

Hammer: A literal hammer; natural or supernatural force; a weapon; God's word; Babylon. (Jer 23:29; Jer 50:23; Judg 4:21.)

Hand: Strength; authority; power; provision; the cause of an action; giving or taking; oath; works; invitation; direction; help; welcome; covenant; agreement; opposition; to harm. (Gen 3:22; Gen 4:11; Gen 5:29; Gen 9:2; Gen 14:22.)

Harp: Praise or worship to God; a joyful heart; to talk persistently on a topic. (1 Sam 16:23; Ps 33:2 Isa 16:11; Isa 24:8; Rev 5:8.)

Harvest: Reaping; the consequences of one's actions; the fruit of evangelism; the judgment of nations at the end of the age. (Gen 8:22; Prov 10:5; Isa 18:5; Jer 12:13; Joel 3:13; Matt 9:37-38; Matt 13:30-39.)

Hat: Authority; identity; covering; role or responsibility; honor or dishonor. (Gen 49:26; Ex 29:4-6; 2 Sam 12:30; Isa 28:1-5; Isa 59:17; Ps 21:3; Rev 3:11.)

Hay: A thing of little value; the fleeting existence of man; works done out of wrong motives. (Isa 40:8; Matt 6:30; 1 Cor 3:12-13; 1 Pet 1:24.)

Head: Authority; Christ; seat of power; husband or father; spiritual leader; government; countenance; self-image. (Gen 3:15; Gen 40:13; Job 2:12; Job 10:16; Job 20:6; Prov 16: 31; Isa 9:15; 1 Cor 11:3.)

Heart: One's true identity, personality, desires, or motives; one's innermost thoughts; the human spirit or soul; the seat of faith, hope, will, and emotion; the conscience; the altar of true worship to God. (Gen 6:5-6; Gen 17:17; Gen 43:30; Ex 9:7; Job 15:12; Ps 7:10; Jer 4:19;

Gal 4:6; 2 Cor 1:22; 2 Cor 3:3; Eph 5:19; 1 Tim 1:5; Heb 4:12; Heb 10:16; 1 Pet 3:4; 1 John 3:20-21.)

Hedge: Protection; confinement; wall. (Job 1:10; Ps 80:12; Ps 89:40; Mark 12:1.)

Helicopter: Able to move freely in all directions; ascending or descending; angelic being; Christ; ministry of rescue (salvation). (Gen 28:12; Gen 22:11; Ex 14:19; Ezek 1:19-21; Ezek 8:3.)

Helmet: Protection for the mind against the schemes of the enemy; salvation. (Isa 59:17; Eph 6:17; 1 Thess 5:8.)

Hen (see chicken)

Highway: The path of God; a path of destiny for man ordained by God; the path of righteousness; a well-traveled path; a safe or easy path; the traditions of man; highway to heaven; road to destruction. (Num 20:17; Prov 15:19; Prov 16:17; Isa 35:8; Isa 40:3; Jer 18:15; Matt 7:13.)

Hill: The habitation of God; the dwelling place of God's people; elevated position for military conflict; prosperity; protection; holy; heavenly; ancient; eternal; pride; arrogance; a place of idol worship. (Gen 49:26; Deut 33:15; Ps 2:6; 1 Sam 23:19; 1 Sam 26:3; Isa 30:17; Isa 40:4; Isa 41:15; Ezek 6:13; Matt 5:14.)

Honey: Source of strength, power or wisdom; the enlightenment of the Holy Spirit; source of knowledge; God's word; divine provision, abundance or blessing; a pleasant experience; enticement; empty words. (Ex 3:8; Judges 14:8-9; Ps 19:10; Ps 119:103; Prov 5:3; Prov 16:24; Isa 7:22; Rev 10:9-10.)

Horn: Divine or human governmental rulership; Christ; seat of power; strength; alarm; pride. (Ps 18:2; Ps 75:4-5; Ps 75:10; Ps 89:17; Ps 98:6; Jer 48:25; Ezek 29:21; Dan 7:7-24; Dan 8:5-22; Zech 1:18-21.)

Hornet: Instrument of God; evil spirit. (Ex 23:2.)

Horse: Power; swiftness; wealth; military might; the strength (or weakness) of man's devices; harbinger of judgment. (Ex 15:1; Deut 17:16; Deut 20:1; Ps 20:7; Ps 33:17; Isa 5:28; Isa 30:16; Rev 6:2-8.)

Hospital: The church; the ministry of healing. (Matt 4:24; Matt 9:12; Luke 4:23.)

Hotel: Temporary station in life; a time of transition; a time (or place) of rest. (Gen 32:13; Josh 2:1; Josh 6:11; Luke 2:7; Luke 10:34-35; Matt 21:17; Acts 10:23.)

House: One's thoughts, motives and actions; the heart, spirit or soul; the human body; the church; one's natural or spiritual family; ministry or business; eternal dwelling place. (Gen 7:1; Gen 12:1; Job 4:19; Job 17:13; Prov 2:18; Prov 7:27; Prov 9:14; Prov 24:3; John 14:2; Rev 21:10-23.)

Husband: Natural husband; Christ; God the Father; spiritual leader. (Isa 62:5; Matt 9:15; Matt 25:1-10; Rev 22:17.)

··· I ···

Ice: The breath of God; hard; cold; deceitful; dark. (Job 6:15-16; Job 37:10; Job 38:29-30.)

Incense: Sacrifice; prayer; intercession; worship of God or idols. (Ex 30:1; Jer 1:16; Ps 141:2; Rev 8:3-4.)

Insurance: Assurance of salvation; faith or confidence; preparedness; safety; divine protection; sealed. (Gen 22:16; Ex 12:7; Rom 8:11; Eph 1:13; Rev 5:1-5.)

Iron (metal): Strength; rulership; impenetrability; inferiority; the systems and governments of man. (Lev 26:19; Job 40:18; Job 41:27; Dan 2:33-45; Rev 2:27.)

Island: Independent; a person; a nation; a distant location. (Ps 97; Isa 11:11; Isa 40:15-17; Isa 66:19; Rev 16:20.)

Ivory: Strength; beauty; wealth. (1 Kings 10:18; Ps 45:8; Ezek 27:15; Amos 3:15.)

··· J ···

Jet airplane: Powerful ministry; ministry to a small number of people (the size of the aircraft may indicate the size of the ministry).

Jewelry: A thing of value; a sign of honor; salvation; worldly wisdom; idolatry; (Isa 54:12; Isa 61:10; Ezek 16:11; Ps 73:6; Prov 8:11; Prov 16:16; Job 28:12-19; Rev 18:12-17.)

Judge: Earthly judge; God the Father; Christ; arbiter of justice. (Ex 18:13; Job 21:22; Dan 7:9-10; Isaiah 11:3-4; Rev 19:11-13.)

··· K ···

Key: Authority; opportunity; access; knowledge; power; wisdom; life or death; (Isa 22:22; Matt 16:19; Luke 11:52; Rev 1:18.)

King: Rulership; authority; Christ. (Dan 2:37; Mark 15:2; Rev 17:14.)

Kiss: Greeting or farewell; meeting or joining; covenant; agreement; anointing; enticement; seduction; deception; betrayal. (Gen 27:26; 1 Sam 10:1; 1 Kings 19:18; Ps 85:10 Ps 2:12; Prov 27:6; Luke 22:47-48; Rom 16:16.)

Kitchen: A place of preparation, particularly of spiritual nourishment; the human soul or spirit.

Knee: Submission; surrender; praise; worship; comfort; strength or weakness. (Gen 41:43; 1 Kings 8:54; 1 Kings 19:18; 2 Kings 4:20; Job 4:4; Isa 35:3; Ps 109:24.)

Knife: Words; judging truth from falsehood; threat or intimidation; fear. (Prov 30:14; Ps 52:2; Isa 54:17; Heb 4:12.)

··· L ···

Ladder: To ascend or descend; to move in the heavenly realm; promotion or demotion. (Gen 28:12-13; John 1:51; John 3:13.)

Lake: The world; a place of ministry; a place of trial or testing; a place of God's peace; a place of judgment. (Mark 3:7; Mark 4:1; Mark 4:39; Matt 8:24-27; Matt 13:47; Rev 19:20.)

Lamb: Innocence; sacrifice or offering; the believer; Christ. (Gen 22:7-8; Ex 29:38-39; Isa 40:11; Isa 53:7; Luke 10:3; John 1:29; John 21:15; Rev 5:1-13.)

Lamp: Spiritual light; the Holy Spirit; the church; the word of God; wisdom; the heart, spirit or soul; the eye. (Ex 25; 2 Sam 22:29; Job 12:5; Job 21:17; Ps 119:105; Prov 6:23; Prov 20:27; Matt 5:15; Matt 6:22; Matt 25:1-8; Rev 1:12-20; Rev 4:5.)

Laundry: Purification; cleansing; (Mal 3:2; Zech 3:3-4.)

Law: The Bible; civil or criminal code; the Old Testament; the books of Moses; the human heart; the human spirit; religious legalism. (Ex 20:2-17; Jer 31:33; John 7:23; Gal 2:16.)

Lawyer (see attorney)

Leaf: Life; eternal life; healing; newness; covering sin; abundance or prosperity. (Gen 3:7; Prov 11:28; Rev 22:2.)

Leash/collar: To control or to be controlled.

Leech: Someone (or something) that drains the life out of others; a parasitic condition; a demonic attachment. (Prov 30:15.)

Left: Riches; honor; foolishness; weakness; subservience; (Gen 48:14-20; Prov 3:16; Eccl 10:2; Matt 25:33.)

Leg: Support; strength; one's spiritual walk. (Gen 32:25-32; Prov 26:7; Song 5:15; Ps 1:1; Gal 5:25.)

Leopard: Swiftness; cunning; predatory; instrument of judgment; principality; human ruler. (Jer 5:6; Dan 7:6; Hos 13:7; Hab 1:8; Rev 13:2.)

Letter: Message; divine revelation; testimony; instruction; the believer; (Ex 17:14; Ex 34:1; Isa 8:1; Luke 1:3; 2 Cor 3:2; Rev 1:11.)

Library: Heaven's repository of information and history; the pursuit of knowledge; the pursuit of wisdom or instruction; study or research. (Gen 5:1; Ex 32:32; Ps 56:8; Dan 7:10; Rev 20:12.)

License: Authority; identity; permission; seal of approval; sign of competence. (Est 8:8; Titus 3:12-13; Luke 9:1; Luke 10;19; Rev 14:1.)

Lifeguard: Christ; the Holy Spirit; an angel; spiritual leader. (Gen 45:7; Ex 2:6; Ex 14:21-22; Acts 16:31; Acts 27:43-44.)

Light: God the Father; the Holy Spirit; Christ; the word of God; the glory of God; divine enlightenment, revelation or illumination; the church; the human spirit; truth; the path of righteousness. (Ex 25:37; 2 Sam 22:29; Ps 18:28; Ps 119:105; Prov20:27; John 1:4-7; 1 Tim 6:16; Rev 1:20.)

Lightning: Swiftness; the power of God; the glory of God; judgment; falling. (Ex 19:16; Dan 10:6; Ezek 1:13; Ps 77:18; Matt 24:27; Matt 28:3; Luke 10:18; Rev 4:5.)

Lily: Beauty; purity; love; God; mankind. (Song 2:1-2; Song 2:16; Hos 14:5; Matt 6:28.)

Lion: Royal authority; the face of God; Christ; Satan; an angel; strength; confidence; bravery; vigilance; cunning; pride; an enemy; instrument of judgment; one who waits in ambush. (Gen 49:9; Num 23:24; Jud 14:18; 1 Kings 13:24-26; Job 28:8; Ps 22:13; Prov 28:1; Isa 21:8; Lam 3:10; Dan 7:4; 1 Pet 5:8; Rev 4:7; Rev 5:5; Rev 13:2.)

Lips: Words or speech; prayer; vow; praise; laughter; rejoicing; wisdom; foolishness; wickedness; slander; deceit; flattery; seduction. (Deut 23:23;

Isa 28:11; Job 8:21; Job 27:4; Ps 63:3; Ps 120:2; Ps 141:3; Prov 4:24; Prov 5:2-3; Prov 14:3; Prov 16:27; Heb 13:15.)

Living room: A literal room in a house; the location in dreams where information about relationships is conveyed.

Lizard: Evil spirit; Satan. (Rev 12:9.)

Lock: Security; safety; caution; admitted or denied access; puzzle; frustration; impatience. (Gen 24:60; Judges 3:23; Job 21:9; Ps 144:2.)

Locker: The human heart or soul. (1 Chron 28:9; Ps 142:7; Isa 61:1.)

Log: Weakness; fault; sin. (Matt 7:3.)

Lottery: Gambling; risk; divine providence. (Matt 17:27.)

··· M ···

Machine: The process of creation or fabrication; productivity; ingenuity; efficiency; automation; manmade mechanism (as opposed to divinely created life); the strength and wisdom of man; reliance on man. (Eccl 7:29; Matt 12:36; Romans 7:5.)

Mailbox: The human heart or soul; the mind; a repository of divine messages; communication. (Ezek 3:10; 2 Kings 10:1-2; Jer 29:1; 2 Cor 3:2-3; Rev 1:11.)

Makeup: To beautify; covering for sin; concealment; pretentious or shallow; deceptive; to reconcile (make up). (Jer 4:30; Ezek 23:40; 2 Kings 9:30; Matt 23:27.)

Man: A man who appears in a dream or vision may represent the person they appear to be, or another person. The demeanor of the man, his words, actions and appearance are clues to who he represents. Sometimes an old man represents our old ways. A young man might represent the dreamer at a young age. A father may represent God, the Father. Christ and heavenly angels frequently appear as men, as do fallen angels and evil spirits. The color and style of clothing a man wears and a vehicle they use can provide further clues to their identity. (Gen 6:4; Gen 19:1; Dan 7:4; Dan 7:9; Dan 8:15-17; Gen 31:11; Zech 3:1-3; Job 1: 6-7; Heb 13:2; Josh 5:13-14.)

Mansion: A representation of one's spiritual life; one's heavenly home; the human heart; the temple of God; the church. (Ezek 40:5; John 14:2; 2 Cor 5:1; Heb 9:11.)

Mantle: Spiritual position of authority; God's anointing; prophetic office. (1 Sam 28:14; 1 Kings 19:13-19; 2 Kings 2:5-14.)

Map: Big picture view of events; divine blueprint; strategy for success; direction in life; instruction on how to reach one's divine destiny; course correction; the word of God. (Dan 9:22-27; 1 Sam 10:3-8; Judg 18:5-6; Luke 9:22.)

Marriage: Natural marriage; spiritual covenant; the church as the Bride of Christ; devotion to God; agreement; partnership (whether good or bad); bondage; idolatry. (Isa 61:10; Hos 4:13-14; Matt 22:1-13; 1 Cor 7; 2 Cor 6:14; Rev 19:6-8.)

Mask: Two-faced; hypocrisy; inauthentic; insincere; concealment; deception. (Gen 27:15-16; Gen 38:14-15; Matt 7:15; Matt 26:25.)

Maze: A setting where one feels lost and uncertain, usually implying a need for divine guidance.

Meal: Spiritual intimacy; receiving spiritual nourishment; fellowship with others. (Matt 26:26; Acts 2:46.)

Meat: Sound teaching; performing God's will. (John 4:34; 1 Cor 3:2; Heb 5:12.)

Mechanic: One who helps others; the Holy Spirit; Christ; prophet, pastor, or counselor; the ministry of healing. (Matt 8:3; John 14:15-16; Acts 15:32; Acts 16:6-8.)

Medicine: A health problem; divine healing; under the influence of a spell; sorcery; witchcraft; addiction; control; rebellion; deception;

religious legalism; sin. (Jer 8:22; Jer 30:13; Prov 17:22; Rev 9:21 (pharmakeia); Gal 3:1.)

Meteor: Divine message or messenger; judgment. (Mat 24:29; Rev 6:13; Rev 8:10.)

Microphone: Amplifies one's voice; spiritual authority; influence. (Matt 10:27; Mark 4:1; 1 Cor 16:9; Acts 4:8.)

Microscope: Used to inspect that which is not normally visible; careful research; discernment; self-examination; nit-picking; obsessing over irrelevant details; micromanagement. (Matt 23:24; 1 Cor 11:28; 1 Cor 12:10; Rev 2:23.)

Microwave Oven: Immediate results; convenience; impatience. (Matt 8:14-15; James 1:3-4.)

Midnight: The hour when a situation may suddenly change; the hour of repentance; the time when men seek God; the beginning of the third watch; the hour of judgment. (Ex 12:29; Judg 16:3; Matt 25:6; Mark 13:35; Luke 11:5.)

Milk: Spiritual nourishment; blessing or abundance; spiritual immaturity. (Ex 3:8; Heb 5:21-13.)

Mirror: The word of God; the human heart; one's conscience; examining oneself; looking at one's past; memories; vanity. (1 Cor 13:12; Prov 27:19; James 1:23-25.)

Miscarriage: A literal miscarriage; to abort against one's will; unexpected cancellation; unjust judgment (miscarriage of justice); failure; sudden loss. (2 Sam 12:16-23; Hab 1:4; Isa 47:11; Jer 6:26.)

Missile: Powerful spiritual weapon: deadly accuracy; powerful ministry; swiftness; unseen attack; spiritual warfare. (1 Sam 17:49; 2 Kings 1:10; Ps 64:7; Prov 6:15.)

Money: Natural wealth; God's glory; divine provision; heavenly or earthly power; spiritual or temporal authority; natural talent or skill; spiritual gifting; faith; wisdom; the price of redemption; the price of betrayal; the strength of man; covetousness or greed. (Deut 8:18; Deut 28:12; Luke 19:23; 1 Tim 6:10; Eccl 7:12; Matt 13:44; Matt 27:3-5 Mark 10:21-22; Luke 16:11; 1 Cor 6:20; Rev 3:17.)

Monkey: Child-like; immature; mischievous; foolish; addiction ("monkey on his back"); clinging. (Job 18:3; Psalm 49:20; Ps 73:22; 2 Pet 2:12.)

Moon: Mother or sister; the church; the occult; idolatry; changes in the appearance of the moon are a sign of the impending return of Christ. (Gen 37:9-10; Deut 4:19; Luke 21:25-27; Rev 12:1.)

Moth: Decay; destruction; rottenness; judgment; fleeting existence. (Job 4:19; Job 13:28; Isa 50:9; Hos 5:12; Matt 6:19-20.)

Mother-in-law: Natural mother-in-law; one who offers help or advice; meddler; religious legalism. (Ruth 2:19-22; Ruth 3:1-4.)

Mother: Spiritual or natural mother; the Holy Spirit; Eve; Israel; the church; one who nurtures; one who commits spiritual adultery. (Gen 3:20; Gal 4:29; Isa 50:1; Matt 23:37; Rev 2:21-23.)

Motor (see engine)

Motorcycle: Unconventional ministry; individual ministry; powerful ministry.

Mountain: The kingdom of God; heaven; to commune with God; the glory of God; a position of spiritual authority; a place of safety; conse-cration to God; a place of prayer; a stronghold; a nation; an obstacle; ancient; pride; place of idolatry; instrument of judgment. (Gen 8:4; Gen 19:17; Ex 3:1; Ex 3:12; Ex 15:17; Josh 14:12; 2 Kings 19:23; Ps 72:3; Ps 90:2; Isa 40:4; Jer 3:6; Matt 4:8; Matt 14:23; Matt 17:20; Mark 9:2; Rev 8:8; Rev 17:9.)

Mouse: Small or insignificant; hidden; timid; judgment; evil spirit. (1 Sam 6:4-5; Lev 11:29.)

Mouth: The human heart; passion; bearing witness; confession of faith; to preach; to accuse; to be silent; to make a vow; to proclaim divine judgment; blaspheme; destruction. (Gen 4:11; Ex 4:12; Num 16:30; Num 22:38; Num 30:2; Deut 31:19; Judg 18:19; Eccl 5:6; Song 7:9; Isa 49:2; Isa 55:11; Matt 12:34; Matt 15:11; Matt 18:16; Acts 15:7; Rom 10:8-10; Rev 1:16; Rev 13:5; Rev 19:21.)

Movie: A literal film the dreamer may be involved with; an illustration of one's life story or part of it; memories; future events; the revelation of one's divine destiny; film titles sometimes contain symbolic messages from God. (1 Sam 10:1-8; Jer 1:5.)

Moving: Change in life circumstances i.e., church, job, or residence. (Gen 12:1-4; Ezek 12:3.)

Mud: Humanity; humility; on slippery or precarious footing; stuck; sinking; down-trodden; (Job 10:9; Mic 7:10; Ps 40:2; John 9:6.)

Museum: One's past; notable achievements; memories; ancient ways; religious traditions; dead religion. (1 Kings 11:41; Luke 1:1-2; John 21:25; Heb 1:1-2; Heb 11; Rev 3:1.)

Mushroom: Sudden growth; fragile; deception; deadly poison. (Jonah 4:10.)

Music: Worship or praise of God; celebration; victory; idolatry. (Ex 15:21; Ex 32:18; 1 Sam 18:6; 2 Sam 6:5; Isa 14:11; Eph 5:19; Rev 5:9.)

Musical Instrument: Ministry of praise and worship; revelation of musical talent; ministry of deliverance; prophecy. (Ezek 28:13; 2 Kings 3:14-17; 1 Chron 25:1; 1 Sam 10:5; 1 Sam 16:23.)

··· **N** ···

Nail (carpenter's): Secure; steadfast; penetrating; finished work; piercing words. (Eccl 12:11; Jer 10:4; Col 2:14.)

Naked: Transparent; honest; innocent; bold; vulnerable; unprepared; spiritually unclothed; natural or spiritual poverty; ashamed; sensuality; sin. (Gen 2:25; Gen 3:7-10; 1 Sam 19:24; Job 24:10; Job 26:6; Isa 20:4; Ezek 16:36-37; 2 Cor 5:2-4; Rev 3:17.)

Name: When you know the name of a person or place in a dream, the meaning of the name may be the primary message. Look up the meaning. (A list of names with their meanings is provided in the last chapter). The meaning of a name may suggest something about one's identity, calling, talent, gifting or an aspect of their character. Sometimes, a minister with a name you recognize will appear in a dream and God may call to you to a similar ministry. (Gen 17:19; Gen 25:26; Gen 26:22; Gen 32:27-28; Isa 62:4; Luke 1:13-17; Matt 1:21; John 1:42.)

Nation: The meaning of a nation that appears in a dream or vision is usually personal to the dreamer. It sometimes indicates a ministry opportunity for the dreamer in that nation. (Ezek 11:24-25; Matt 2:13-15; Matt 2:19-23; Acts 16:9.)

Neck: The human will; decision-making; bearing a burden; a point of weakness or vulnerability; a narrowing; strength; victory; sensuality; stubborn; pride; unbelief; death. (Gen 49:8; Deut 21:4; Jer 17:23; 2 Sam 22:41; Job 41:22; Song 4:4.)

Necklace: Gift; sacrifice or offering; a willing heart; servanthood; sensuality; pride; bondage. (Ex 35:22; Num 31:50; Ps 73:6; Song 4:9.)

Neighbor: Someone in need; a friend; an angel; an unbeliever. (Prov 3:28; Prov 3:29; Eph 2:19; Matt 19:19; Luke 10:36; Heb 13:2.)

Nest: Home; bed; safety; security (real or false); a place or time of rest. (Num 24:21; Deut 32:11; Job 39:27; Obad 1:4; Matt 8:20.)

Net: Ministry of evangelism; the kingdom of God; trap; seduction; deception; evil motives; the internet. (Prov 29:5; Eccl 7:26; Eccl 9:12; Luke 5:5-6; Matt 13:47.)

News (newspaper): Divine revelation; prophecy; preaching; teaching; communicating with the public; gossip; propaganda. (1 Sam 4:19; 2 Sam 18:25; Prov 25:25; Isa 52:7; Isa 61:1; Ezek 21:7; Luke 8:17; Matt 10:27.)

Night: Fading glory; time when Christ is not physically present on the earth; a time when the works of darkness are done; the end of life. (Gen 29:23; Ps 59:6; Prov 7:9-13; Rom 13:12; 1 Thess 5:5-7; Rev 22:5.)

Nine: Fruitfulness; fruit of the Spirit; spiritual gifts. (Gen 17:1-2; Gal 5:22-23; 1 Cor 12:4-10.)

North: God's throne; the heavenly kingdom; the mountain of God. (Job 26:7; Job 37:22; Ps 48:2; Isa 14:13; Ezek 1:4.)

Nose: Sensitivity to spiritual matters; how one is led (nose ring or follow your nose); persistent, unrelenting or stubborn (hard-nosed); proud or offended (turned up nose). Isa 37:29; Isa 65:5; Job 27:3.)

Nurse: The Holy Spirit; Christ; an angel; healing minister; nurturer. (John 14:16-18; Mark 1:13; Acts 3:6.)

··· O ···

Oak: Strength; stability; longevity; the kingdom of God; shelter; pride; idolatry. (Isa 2:12-13; Isa 6:13; Amos 2:9; Ezek 6:13.)

Ocean: The world and its inhabitants (nations); the knowledge of God; righteousness; ferociousness; the wicked; resting place of the dead; route of commerce; double-mindedness. (Gen 1:10; Gen 14:3; Isa 11:9; Isa 17:12; Isa 48: Isa 57:20; Ezek 27:33; Dan 7:3; Matt 8:26; Matt 13:47; 1 Cor 10:1-2; James 1:6; Rev 10:2; Rev 13:1; Rev 15:2; Rev 20:13.)

Octopus: Controlling spirit. (1 Kings 21:7-8; Rev 14:8-9.)

Office: Pertaining to business or commerce; pertaining to the work of God's kingdom; spiritual office or position, i.e., apostle, prophet, pastor, teacher, or evangelist. (Dan 2:49; Eph 4:11-12; 1 Cor 15:9.)

Oil: God's anointing; God's glory; the Holy Spirit; spiritual light or life; ministry of healing; unclean spirit (dirty oil); seduction; deception. (Gen 28:18; Ex 30:22-30; Ps 55:21; Prov 5:3; Mark 6:13; James 5:14; Matt 25:3-8.)

Old house: One's life before Christ; traditions or customs (whether good or bad); ancestors; memories. (Job 8:8; Job 15:28; Eccl 1:11; 2 Cor 5:1-4; Heb 10:32; 1 Pet 3:5; Rev 21:4.)

Old man: Natural father or grandfather; God the Father; one's life before Christ; old ways of thinking; old habits; wisdom; ancestor. (Dan 7:9-10; Job 12:12; Prov 16:31; Eph 4:17-24; Rom 6:6; 1 Cor 13:11; Titus 2:1-2.)

Old Woman: Natural mother or grandmother; the church; the Holy Spirit; one's life before Christ; old ways of thinking; old habits; wisdom; ancestor. (Prov 14:1; Eph 4:17-24 Rom 6:6 1 Cor 13:11; Titus 2:3-5.)

Olive (olive tree): God's anointing; an anointed person; the two witnesses of Revelation chapter 11; fruit of the Spirit; Israel; the believer; descendants. (Ex 30:22-30; Ps 52:8; Ps 128:3; Isa 17:6; Jer 11:16; Zech 4:11-14; Rev 11:3-6.)

One: Origin; beginning; God as the source; first chronologically; of primary importance; unique; solitary. (Deut 6:4; John 1:1-3; Matt 8:20; James 2:19; 1 Tim 2:5.)

One Hundred: Fullness. (Matt 13:23; Matt 19:29; Luke 15:4.)

Orange: Warning; emergency; power.

Oven: The human heart; the womb; sign of God's covenant; adversity; refiner; seat of passion; judgment; idolatry. (Gen 15:17; Dan 3:19-25; Hos 7:4-7; Mal 4:1; Ps 21:9; 1 Cor 7:9.)

Owl: Wisdom; evil spirit; solitude; loneliness; desolation. (Isa 13:21; Isa 34:11; Ps 102:6.)

Ox: The face of God; strength; possessions or wealth; servanthood; sacrifice; idol; foolishness. (Gen 12:16; Ex 20:24; Ex 32:4; Job 1:3; Prov 7:21-23; Ezek 1:10.)

··· **P** ···

Painting (noun): Divine revelation regarding a subject; likeness or representation of something or someone; an abstraction; visualization; an idol. (Gen 1:26-27; Gen 5:3; Lev 26:1; Dan 2:31; Rev 13:14-15.)

Painting (verb): Creative endeavor; prophetic revelation; divine calling; inward renewal; outward refurbishment; covering one's flaws; hypocrisy. (Matt 23:27; Ex 31:6; 2 Kings 9:30; 1 Sam 16:7; Jer 22:14; 2 Cor 4:16; 2 Cor 4:16; 1 Pet 3:3-4.)

Palace: Dwelling place of royalty (both heavenly and earthly). The center of God's kingdom; the place of God's presence; the believer's home in heaven; seat of authority; spiritual or natural blessing or abundance; pride. (Est 2:13; Ps 45:13; Ps 122:7; 2 Chron 36:19; 2 Kings 20:18; Luke 11:21; John 14:2; Rev 21.)

Palm Tree: Triumph; worship; rejoicing; holiness; the city of Jericho; (Lev 23:40; 1 Kings 6:29; 2 Chron 28:15; John 12:13; Rev 7:9.)

Parachute: Heavenly message; angelic messenger; spiritual warfare; arrival of reinforcements; rescue operation; safety net; backup plan; the will to survive. (Gen 28:12; Josh 2:14-15; Matt 2:13; Acts 9:25; Acts 12:7.)

Paramedic: Ministry of healing; Christ; the Holy Spirit; an angel. (Judg 6:21; John 5:4; Mark 1:30-32.)

Passenger: Surrender to God; being controlled by others; riding in a vehicle with a faceless driver may indicate being led by the Holy Spirit. (Deut 5:32; John 21:18; Rom 8:14.)

Pasture: Place of rest and refreshing; place of spiritual nourishment; the habitation of God's people; the church. (1 Chron 4:40; Ps 23:1-2; Ps 79:13; John 21:17).

Path: The intentions of the heart; one's choices, preferences, habits or decisions (whether good or bad); personal relationship with God; divine destiny; the future; the way of salvation; career choice. (Jer 6:16; Isa 35:8; Isa 42:16; Ps 23:3; Prov 2:8; Prov 2:18; Prov 3:6; Matt 7:13-14.)

Peacock: The living creatures of Revelation chapter 4; pride; narcissism. (2 Chron 9:21 (KJV); Rom 1:23; 1 Cor 13:4; Rev 4:6.)

Pearl: The believer; the church; service to God; Christ; wisdom; faith; the gates of the heavenly Jerusalem; false religion. (Matt 7:6; Matt 13:45-46; Luke 12:33; Col 2:3; 1 Cor 3:12-13; Rev 17:4; Rev 18:12.)

Pelican: Solitude; independence; loneliness. (Ps 102:6; Zeph 2:14.)

Pen/pencil: Communication; divine revelation; inspiration; thoughts or words; the heart; contract; vow; publish; record; testify. (Ex 17:14; Ex 34:1; Prov 3:3; Ps 45:1; Jer 31:33; Ezek 3:1; Luke 1:1-3; Rev 21:5.)

Perfume: God's presence; angelic presence; anointing; sacrifice; influence or persuasion; seduction; deception. (Ex 30:25; Prov 7:17-18; Eccl 10:1; Mark 14:3; Eph 5:2.)

Photograph: Identity; divine revelation; divine calling; testimony; memory; emotional scar; idol. (Gen 1:27; Gen 28:18-19; Ex 20:4; Ex 28:21; Dan 2:31; Ps 73:19-21; 1 Cor 15:49; 2 Cor 3:18.)

Pickpocket: Natural thief; spiritual identity thief (evil spirit); spirit of sickness; seduction; deception. (Prov 7:22-23; John 10:10; Gal 3:1.)

Pierced ear: Servanthood; loyalty; slavery; bondage. (Ex 21:6; Eph 6:5-6; Gal 5:1; Jude 1:1.)

Pig: Unbeliever; foolish; lacking discretion; demon-possessed. (Lev 11:7; Prov 11:22; Matt 7:6; Matt 8:31-32.)

Pigeon: Sacrifice; poverty. (Lev 5:7.)

Pillar: The believer; Christ; the Holy Spirit; angel of God; God's glory; memorial; tombstone; strength; wisdom; reliability; loyalty; disloyalty;

idolatry. (Gen 19:26; Gen 28:18; Ex 13:21; Ex 14:19; Ex 23:24; Ex 33:9; Prov 9:1; Song 5:15; Gal 2:9; Rev 3:12.)

Pillow: Christ; rest. (Gen 28:10-18; Matt 8:20.)

Pilot: The Holy Spirit; the thoughts and intentions of the heart; one's motives or desires; the soul. (Ps 31:3; Prov 3:5-6; John 14:16-17.)

Pink: Feminine; chaste; innocent; sensual; immoral.

Pit (hole): Life circumstance; divinely ordained situation; trap; depression; consequence of sin; judgment. (Gen 37:18-24; Gen 50:20; Ps 7:14-15; Ps 35:7; Ps 40:2; Ps 55:23; Ps 69:15.)

Pitcher: The heart or soul; vessel of the Holy Spirit. (Jer 18:6; Phil 2:17; Rom 9:21; 2 Cor 4:7)

Plant (verb): To be established by God; sharing the gospel; discipleship; (Isa 55:10; Isa 60:21; Isa 61:3; Matt 13:18-19; 1 Cor 3:5-8.)

Playing: Childlike innocence; recreation; immaturity. (Matt 11:16-18; 1 Cor 13:11.)

Plow: A tool used to prepare ground for planting (preparing hearts to receive God's love); breaking new ground (pioneering and innovation) breaking hard ground (overcoming stubbornness); servanthood; labor; sin. (1 Sam 8:12; 1 Kings 19:19; Job 4:8; Prov 20:4; Luke 9:62.)

Plumber: Christ; the Holy Spirit; a believer operating in the gift of helps. (Isa 44:3; Zech 4:11-14; John 4:10-14; 1 Cor 12:28.)

Plumbline: Instrument of divine measure; discerning good from evil or right from wrong; divine judgment. (Amos 7:7-9 Zech 4:10.)

Police: Natural or spiritual authority; one who enforces natural or spiritual laws; protector; agent of divine judgment (angel); one who enforces religious legalism. (Num 22:22-23; Matt 22:21; Rom 3:19-20; Rom 13:1-7; Rev 12:7-9.)

Pomegranate: Fruit of the Spirit; priesthood; consecration to God; (Ex 39:24-36; 1 Kings 7:18-20; 1 Kings 7:20; Isa 32:15; Matt 3:10; Gal 5:22.)

Porch: A porch attached to the front of a house illustrates the future; attached to the rear of the house, it signifies the past. (Rev 4:1-3.)

Portal: Path through which we receive divine revelation; access to heaven; passageway to the kingdom of God. (2 Kings 2:11; Ezek 1:4-5; John 6:21; Acts 8:39-40; Rev 4:1-3.)

Postage stamp: Seal; authorization; seemingly insignificant, but powerful. (Est 8:8; John 6:27; Rev 5:1-2)

Power line: The power of God at work; the way in which God disseminates His messages; the believer. (Luke 8:45-47; Matt 10:27; Acts 8:25.)

Precious stone: A thing of value; the tribes of Israel; Christ; the believer; the believer's works; spiritual gift; foundation; idolatry. (Ex 28:17-21; Isa 28:16; 1 Cor 3:12; 1 Pet 2:4; Rev 21:11; Rev 17:4.)

Pregnancy: Natural pregnancy; incubating a divinely appointed ministry, career, relationship or other matter; promise; expectancy; anticipating the arrival of something (whether good or bad). Isa 66:7-9; James 1:15; Mark 13:8; Rev 12:1-5.)

Priest: Christ; the believer; church leader; Melchizedek; religious spirit; idolater. (Gen 14:18; Ex 28:41; 2 Kings 10:18-19; Heb 6:20; 1 Pet 2:5; Rev 1:5-6.)

Prince: Christ; Satan; the believer; natural or spiritual leader; authority; royalty; wealth; integrity. (Isa 9:6; Ps 47:9; Ps 68:27; Ps 118:9; Prov 17:26; John 12:31; Eph 2:2.)

Prison: Physical confinement; character refinement; slave of Christ; the consequence of sin; addiction; mental stronghold; spiritual darkness; demonic influence or possession; divine judgment; sheol; hell. (Gen 39:20-23; Isa 42:7; Isa 53:8; Ps 107:14; Matt 10:28; Luke 8:29; Gal 5:1; 1 Pet 3:19; Philem 1:1; Rev 20:7)

Pulley: A thing that reduces friction; a force multiplier; ingenuity; the Holy Spirit. (Eph 4:32; Col 3:12-13; 2 Tim 4:11; Titus 3:9.)

Pulpit: Calling to public ministry as a pastor, teacher, evangelist, prophet, or apostle; public speaking; sharing the gospel. (Luke 4:16-21; Eph 4:11-12; Acts 4:8-12.)

Puppet: Under the control of another; manipulating spirit; deception; (1 Kings 21:7-8; Acts 16:17-18.)

Puppy: Innocence; friendship; spiritual immaturity; trained follower. (1 Sam 18:31; Cor 3:1; 1 Cor 14:20; Heb 5:12-13.)

Purple: Royalty; wealth; prosperity. (Judg 8:26; Ezek 27:16; Dan 5:29; Mark 15:17.)

Purse: Identity; matters of the heart; finances; that which we value; qualification; citizenship; calling; divine destiny. (Prov 2:1; Jer 1:5; Matt 6:19-21; Matt 12:35; John 12:3-6; Rom 1:1.)

Puzzle: Divine mystery to be solved; revelation in riddle or parable; big picture view; confusion; dilemma. (Prov 25:2; Dan 2:27-28; Mark 4:11; 1 Cor 2:7; Rev 1:20.)

··· Q ···

Queen: Royalty; natural or spiritual authority; divine favor; manipulation; idolatry. (1 Kings 10:13; 1 Kings 19:2; Est 5:1-3; Ps 45:9; Jer 44:17-19.)

Quilt: Divine protection or favor; spiritual authority; covering; the Holy Spirit. (Gen 37:3; 1 Kings 19:19; 2 Kings 2:8; John 14:16.)

··· R ···

Race: Living for Christ; enduring hardship; persistence. (1 Cor 9:24; Heb 12:1; James 1:2-4.)

Raccoon: Individual or spirit that causes mischief; thief; nuisance. (John 12:6.)

Radio: The voice of God; divine revelation; receiving information; sharing or hearing the gospel; the spread of gossip or propaganda. (Prov 6:19; Prov 25:25; Matt 10:27; Acts 8:25.)

Rags: Poverty; self-righteousness; sin. (Prov 23:21; Isa 64:6.)

Railroad track: God's plan; the path of a powerful ministry; tradition, stubbornness or habit. (Prov 26:11; Zech 4:6; Mark 7:9; Acts 5:38-39.)

Rain: The Holy Spirit; God's manifest presence; God's grace; God's provision; divine revelation; spiritual revival; the difficulties of life; divine judgment. (Gen 7:4; Ex 16:13-14; Deut 28:12; Deut 32:2; Isa 55:10; Ezek 38:22; Hos 6:3; Hos 14:5; Matt 5:45; Matt 7:25.)

Rainbow: God's glory; God's covenant; sign of God's promise; angel. (Gen 9:13-5; Ezek 1:28; Rev 4:3; Rev 10:1.)

Ram: Strength; wealth; human king or kingdom; sacrifice or offering; Christ. (Gen 22:13; Gen 31:8-10; Dan 8:3-7; Eph 5:2.)

Ram's horn (see shofar)

Rape: Spirit of control (violating another's will); abuse of authority; spirit of lust; desire for power; betrayal; an evil heart. (2 Sam 13:5-14; Deut 22:25-26; Matt 15:19.)

Rapture: The physical removal of believers from earth; temporarily visiting heaven. (Matt; 24:40-41; Rev 4:1-2.)

Rash: Physical sickness; sin. (Lev 13; 2 Kings 5:9-14; Heb 9:13-14.)

Rat (see mouse)

Raven (see crow)

Receipt: Proof of redemption; seal of the Holy Spirit; the blood of Christ. (John 20:25-27; Eph 1:13-14; Acts 20:28.)

Recycle: Outward change without a change of heart; change brought by man and not God; repetitive behavior. (Ezek 11:19; Mark 2:21-23; Eph 4:23-24.)

Red: Redemption; love; passion; the blood of Christ; sacrifice; warning; anger; sin; idolatry; judgment. (Isa 1:18; Josh 2:18-21; Song 4:3; Rev 12:3; Rev 17:3-4.)

Reed: A weak nation or leader; one who is bruised or afflicted; mock scepter; instrument of measurement. (1 Kings 14:15; 2 Kings 18:21; Isa 42:3; Luke 7:24; Matt 27:29-30; Rev 11:1.)

Reins: Motives of the heart. (Ps 7:9; Jer 17:10.)

Remote control: Mechanical ingenuity; making work easier; laziness; manipulation or control of others; witchcraft. (1 Kings 21:7-8; Acts 16:17-18.)

Reporter: Eyewitness; one who documents events; one who testifies to truth (or falsehood); preacher or evangelist; propagandist. (Luke 1:1-2; 2 Pet 1:16.)

Reservoir: Container of the Holy Spirit (the church or believer); the Holy Spirit in a stagnant state. (Gen 1:9; Ex 17:6; Jer 10:13; John 7:38; Eph 4:30; Rev 7:17; Rev 22:1.)

Restaurant: Communion and fellowship with many people at once; fellowship that breaks from routines and habits; venturing out of one's comfort zone. (Matt 22:10; Matt 26:20; Acts 1:13-14; Rev 19:9.)

Rib: Heart; wife. (Gen 2:21-22; Luke 2:35; John 19:34.)

Rice (see seed)

Rifle (see gun)

Right (direction): Authority; power; preeminence; strength; godliness; longevity. (Gen 48:14-20; Ex 15:6; Prov 3:16; Eccl 10:2; Matt 22:44; Matt 25:33; Matt 26:64.)

Ring: Authority; identity; promise; covenant; eternity (unending); wealth; pride. (Gen 41:42; Est 3:12; Haggai 2:23; James 2:1-3.)

River: The throne of God; the person and work of the Holy Spirit; the river of life; the delineation between life and death; dividing line between faith and unbelief; border or boundary; wisdom; the heart; prosperity and blessing; sign of spiritual renewal or revival. (Gen 2:10; Gen 15:18; Ex 17:6; Ps 1:3; Ps 46:4; Ps 65:9; Prov 18:4; Prov 21:1; Isa 43:19; Ezek 47:3-12; John 7:38; Rev 7:17; Rev 22:1-2.)

Roach: Literal insect infestation; unclean spirit; hidden sin; idolatry. (Lev 11:29; Ezek 8:10.)

Road: The path of God; a path of destiny for man ordained by God; the path of righteousness; a well-traveled path; a safe or easy path; the traditions of man; highway to heaven; road to destruction. (Num 20:17; Prov 15:19; Prov 16:17; Isa 35:8; Isa 40:3; Jer 18:15; Matt 7:13.)

Robe: Royalty; authority; favor; the color of a robe may indicate righteousness or sin; a torn robe indicates astonishment or dismay. (Gen 37:3; Ex 28:4; 2 Sam 13:18-19; 1 Kings 22:10; Est 5:1; Ezra 9:3; Isa 3:24; Isa 6:1; Isa 61:10; Isa 63:3; Zech 3:4; Rev 4:4; Rev 7:14; Rev 19:13.)

Robot: Creative ingenuity; automation; programmed thinking; mind control (brainwashing); religious tradition; habitual behavior; demonic device; heartless. (Gen 19:31-32; 2 Tim 3:3; Rev 13:14-15.)

Rock: God the Father; Christ; reliability; stability; (Ex 17:6; Ex 33:22; Deut 32:4; 2 Sam 22:47; Ps 118:22; Isa 8:14; Isa 28:16; Luke 20:17.) See also stone.

Rocket: Powerful spiritual weapon; deadly accuracy; powerful ministry; swiftness; unseen attack; spiritual warfare. (1 Sam 17:49; 2 Kings 1:10; Ps 64:7; Prov 6:15.)

Roller coaster: Dramatic change; excitement; unpredictable; emotional highs and lows; testing, trial or tribulation; unstable; double-minded. (Isa 40:4; James 1:2-8; Eph 4:14; Acts 27:10; Rev 2:22.)

Roller skates/roller blades: Solo ministry; moving quickly in the spirit; swift advancement; skillful; lacking power; relying on man's strength. (Ps 147:10; Isa 31:1; Jer 12:5; Acts 8:28-30.)

Roof: Protective structure, i.e., church leadership; place of fellowship (permanent or temporary); opportunity to receive divine revelation; highpoint of ministry; preaching platform. (Deut 22:8; Matt 10:27; Acts 10:9-11; Eph 2:19.)

Root: Origin; source; heart; character; ancestors; Christ. (Deut 29:18; 2 Kings 19:30; Job 19:28; Isa 11:10; Dan 4:14-16; Matt 3:10; Matt 13:21.)

Rope/string: Used to bind together (for good or bad); love; unity; rescue or salvation; covenant; promise; influence; dependency; soul tie; spiritual bondage; sin. (1 Sam 18:1; Prov 5:22; Ps 118:27; Josh 2:21; Jer 38:11; Acts 9:25; Eph 4:16; Col 2:2; Gal 5:1.)

Rose: Love; Christ; the church; passion; beauty. (Song 2:1; Isa 35:1-2; 1 Kings 6:29.)

Rowing: Solo ministry; spiritual exercise; work done in man's strength as opposed to the power of the Spirit; striving against God. (Jonah 1:13; Mark 6:48.)

Ruby: Wisdom; virtue; integrity; God's people; a thing of value; (Job 28:18; Prov 3:15; Prov 31:10; Lam 4:7.)

Running: The race of faith; pursuing one's divine destiny; competing in life; strength; the spread of God's word; pursuit of a love interest; searching; contending; haste; fear (whether the cause is real or imagined); demonic attack or harassment; failure to exercise authority; doing evil. (1 Sam 8:11; 2 Chron 16:9; Ps 119:32; Ps 147:15; Prov 1:16; Prov 28:1; Song 1:4; Isa 40:31; Jer 12:5; Jer 49:19; Hab 2:2; 1 Cor 9:24; 1 Cor 9:25-27; Gal 2:2; Heb 12:1.)

Rust: Ancient; decay; laziness; corrupt; greed; worthless. (Eccl 10:18; Matt 6:19-20; James 5:3.)

··· **S** ···

Sail: Powered or led by the Holy Spirit; ministry; voyage. (Luke 8:26; Acts 13:4; Acts 14:26.)

Salt: Godly character; grace; purification; preservation; seasoning; covenant; judgment. (Gen 19:26; Lev 2:13; Deut 29:23; Judg 9:45; Ezek 47:11; Matt 5:13-16; Mark 9:50; Col 4:6.)

Sand: Numerous; hidden; heavy; poor foundation; foolishness; the boundary of the sea. (Gen 22:17; Deut 33:19; Job 6:2-3; Prov 27:3; Jer 5:22; Matt 7:26.)

Sapphire: The throne of God; foundation; Christ; God's people; beauty; a thing of value; the tribes of Israel. (Ex 24:9-10; Song 5:15; Lam 4:7; Ezek 1:26; Rev 21:19.)

Scales (balance): Fairness; equality; justice; truth; worth; divine judgment. (Lev 19:36; Isa 40:12; Dan 5:27; Job 31:6; Mic 6:11; Rev 6:5.)

Scar: Memory; emotional trauma; reminder. (Ps 69:26; Ps 109:22; Song 5:7; Isa 53:5; Isa 61:1; Zech 13:6; Rev 13:3.)

School: Natural school; spiritual instruction; a need for knowledge or wisdom; discipleship; church (whether good or bad); indoctrination. (Ex 18:20; Ps 144:1; Ps 25:9; Mic 3:11; Matt 4:23; Eph 4:11; 1 Cor 2:13; Titus 1:11; Rev 2:20.)

School bus: Teaching ministry. (1 Cor 14:23-33.)

Scooter: Spiritual immaturity; small ministry; lacking power. (1 Cor 14:20; 1 Pet 2:2.)

Scorpion: Desert dweller; stinging words; evil spirit; tormentor; (Ezek 2:6; Luke 10:19; Rev 9:3-5.)

Scroll: The word of God; divine revelation; heavenly plan or blueprint; book of life; journal; written message; the sky. (Ps 40:7; Isa 8:1; Isa 34:4; Ezek 3:2-3; Zech 5:1-3; Rev 5:1-8; Rev 6:14.)

Sea: The oceans; the world and its inhabitants (nations); the knowledge of God; righteousness; the area before God's throne is likened to a sea of glass; ferociousness; the wicked; resting place of the dead; route of commerce; the Red Sea crossing foreshadowed resurrection and baptism; tool of Satan; double-mindedness. (Gen 1:10; Gen 14:3; Ex 14:16; Isa 11:9; Isa 17:12; Isa 48: Isa 57:20; Ezek 27:33; Dan 7:3; Matt 8:26; Matt 13:47; 1 Cor 10:1-2; James 1:6; Rev 10:2; Rev 13:1; Rev 15:2; Rev 20:13.)

Seacoast (coastlands): The region surrounding Tyre and Sidon; the land of Edom. (2 Chron 8:17; Jer 5:22; Jer 25:22; Isa 60:9.)

Seatbelt: Restraint; safety device; angel; the Holy Spirit. (Ex 13:21-22; Num 22:22-27; 2 Thess 2:7.)

Seed: DNA; natural or spiritual offspring; fruit; the word of God; believers; faith; the kingdom of heaven; death and resurrection; Christ. (Gen 1:11; Gen 3:15; Gen 4:25; Gen 21:12; Deut 22:9; 1 Chron 16:13; Ps 89:29; Isa 53:10; Dan 2:43; Matt 13:18-23; Matt 13:24-30; Matt 13:31-32; Matt 13:37-39; Matt 17:20; Rom 1:3; 1 Cor 15:35-44.)

Serpent: Satan; evil spirit; evil person; sin. (Gen 3:1-4; Num 21:8; Ps 58:4; Isa 14:29; Matt 23:33; Luke 10:19; John 3:14; Rev 12:9.)

Seven: Divine completeness and perfection; rest; blessing; divine justice. (Gen 2:2-3; Gen 4:24; Gen 7:4; Gen 41; Rev 1:4; Rev 1:20; Rev 5:1-6; Rev 10:3-4.)

Sewing (knitting): Unite; join; reconcile; repair. (1 Sam 18:1; Eph 4:16; Col 2:2.)

Sex: Procreation; pleasure; love; covenant; fornication; incest; rape; seduction; idolatry; controlled by lust; abuse of authority; conceiving sin. (Gen 4:11; Gen 6:2-4; Gen 19:5; Gen 19:32; Prov 6:25; Ezek 23:7; Rom 1:27; 1 Cor 7:1-9; James 1:15; Rev 2:22.)

Shadow: Shelter; protection; to foreshadow prophetically; time; fleeting; timidity; darkness; death. (Gen 19:8; 2 Kings 20:9-10; Ps 17:8; Ps 91:1 Job 3:5; Job 8:9; Job 14:2; Col 2:17; James 1:17.)

Shark: Predator; devourer; evil spirit; fear; Satan. (Jer 51:34; Ps 17:8-10; Ps 35:16.)

Shaven or unshaven: Holiness; ceremonially clean; consecration to God; strength; grief, mourning or remorse; vow; judgment. (Lev 14:8-9; Num 6:5-9; Judg 13:5; 1 Sam 1:11; Judg 16:17; Isa 7:20; Ezek 5:1-3.)

Sheep: Christ; Disciples of Christ; Israel; sacrifice; innocent; weak; gullible. (John 1:29; John 21:15; Matt 9:36; Matt 10:6; Matt 10:16; Matt 18:12-13; Matt 25:32-33; Rev 5:6-8.)

Shepherd: Christ; natural or spiritual leader (whether good or bad); protector; king; pastor or teacher. (1 Kings 22:17; 1 Chron 11:2; Ps 23:1; Isa 56:11; Matt 7:15; Matt 24:24; 1 Pet 5:1-4.)

Shield: Protection; God; the word of God; the truth; faith; salvation. (Gen 15:1; Ps 3:3; Ps 18:35; Prov 30:5; Eph 6:16.)

Ship: Ministry (size of the ship signifies the size of the ministry); the believer; church; voyage; commerce; wealth; strength; pride; weapon of natural or spiritual warfare. (1 Kings 10:11; Ps 107:23; Isa 2:15-17; Isa 23:14; Jonah 1:3; Matt 8:23; Acts 21:2.)

Shoe/sandal/boot: The gospel; uncleanness; sign of rejection or confirmation. (Ex 3:5; Deut 25:5-10; Eph 6:15; Ruth 4:7-8; Isa 20:2.)

Shofar (ram's horn): Proclamation or announcement; prophetic declaration. (Josh 6:3-11; Hos 5:8.)

Shoulder: Authority; responsibility; load bearing; redeemed; shunned; indifference. (Gen 21:14; Gen 24:45; Gen 49:15; 1 Chron 15:15; Neh 9:29; Isa 9:6; Isa 22:22; Matt 23:4.)

Shower (see bathroom)

Sign: Confirmation; evidence; indicator or signal; miracle; message; instruction; promise or declaration; indicator of change; warning; detour; yield; decision. (Gen 9:12; Ex 4:8; Num 26:10; Hos 12:10; John 2:11; Matt 12:38-40; Matt 24:30; Rev 12:1-3; Rev 13:14.)

Silver: Natural wealth; beauty; redemption; vindication; restitution; offering; glory; refined; second to gold in prominence; the word of God; the cord of life; betrayal; idolatry. (Gen 13:2; Gen 20:16; Gen 37:28; Ex 20:23; Ex 25:3; Ex 21:32; Num 18:16; Dan 2:32; Eccl 12:6; Prov 16:31; Ezek 16:13; Zech 11:13; Matt 27:3-10.)

Silver cord: Spiritual umbilical cord; life and death. (Eccl 12:6.)

Sink (see bathroom)

Sinking: Overwhelm (whether good or bad); trapped; stuck in a rut (habitual behavior); loss of faith (fear); loss of income; loss of ministry; loss of relationship(s); demonic oppression; depravity; judgment; death. (Gen 37:22; Ps 9:15; Ps 30:3; Ps 40:2; Ps 57:6; Prov 22:14; Prov 28:17.)

Sister-in-law (see brother-in-law)

Sister: Natural or spiritual sister; the church; Israel; a friend; wisdom. (Gen 24:60; Ex 15:20; Prov 7:4; Song 4:9; Matt 12:50.)

Six: The likeness of man; human weakness; man's works; labor. (Gen 1:26-31; Ex 16:26; Ex 21:2; Ex 23:10; Lev 25:2-4; Rev 13:18.)

Skateboard: Solo ministry; moving quickly in the spirit; swift advancement; skillful; lacking power; relying on man's strength. (Ps 147:10; Isa 31:1; Jer 12:5; Acts 8:28-30.)

Skeleton: Ancestor; resurrection; spiritual revival; miracle; Israel; evil spirit; judgment; death; (Gen 50:25; 2 Sam 21:13-14; 2 Kings 13:21; Ezek 6:5; Ezek 37:1-14; Matt 23:27.)

Skiing: If skiing on a mountain, it may indicate navigating God's kingdom; individual ministry; moving quickly in the spirit; downhill skiing may indicate moving from a higher (heavenly) to lower (earthly) perspective, or matters becoming worse "things are going downhill"; skillful activity. (Ps 147:10; Isa 31:1; Jer 12:5; Acts 8:28-30.)

Skunk: Individual or spirit that offends; nuisance; hindrance. (Neh 4:3.)

Sky: The heavens or firmament; the habitation of God and His angels; the home of birds; indicator of weather; times and seasons; the glory of God; God's truth, righteousness, justice, faithfulness and mercy; subject to judgment. (Gen 1:7-8; Gen 1:14-20; Isa 34:4; Ps 19:1; Ps 36:5; Ps 97:6; Ps 108:4; Matt 16:2-3; 2 Pet 3:10-13.)

Sleep: Rest; peace; receiving dreams; spiritual activity; resurrection; under anesthesia; spiritually blind; ignorant; inattentive; unaware; lazy; physical death; (Gen 2:21 Gen 28:11-16; Job 4:12-13; Job 33:15-18; Ps 4:8; Ps 13:3; Ps 127:2; Prov 6:9; Eccl 5:12; Isa 29:10; Dan 8:18; Dan 12:2; Matt 9:24; Matt 26:45; Mark 13:35-36; John 11:9-14; Rom 13:11; 1 Cor 11:30; 1 Cor 15:51-52; Eph 5:14; 1 Thess 4:14.)

Smile: God's grace or favor; love; approval; benevolence; seduction. (Num 6:25; Prov 5:3; Prov 15:13; Prov 20:13.)

Smoke: God's presence; sacrifice; prayer; evil spirit; pestilence; judgment; death. (Gen 19:28; Ex 19:18; 2 Sam 22:9; Ps 37:20; Ps 74:1; Song 3:6; Isa 4:5; Rev 8:4; Rev 9:2-3; Rev 14:11 Rev; 15:8.)

Snake (see serpent)

Snow: Pure; righteous; forgiven; new; heavenly; God the Father; Christ; sin; leprosy. (Num 12:10; Ps 51:7; Isa 1:18; Isa 55:10-11; Dan 7:9; Matt 28:3; Rev 1:14.)

Soap: Cleanness; forgiveness; repentance; renewal. (Job 9:30; Ps 26:6; Ps 51:2-7; Isa 1:16; Jer 2:22; Matt 23:26; Matt 27:24; 1 Cor 6:11.)

Soil (see clay)

Soldier/Sniper: The believer; spiritual warfare; evil spirit; an enemy; poverty. (1 Sam 17:40; Ps 12:8; Ps 18:39; Ps 144:1; Prov 6:11; Luke 11:21.)

Son: Natural son; descendant; spiritual son, e.g., a student, disciple, or protege; an angel; Christ; the dreamer at a young age; child of God; one who is born of a woman. (Gen 6:2-4; Ezek 33:2; Dan 7:13; Dan 8:17; Matt 8:20; Rom 8:14; Rev 1:13.)

South: Worldly kingdom (typified by Egypt); whirlwind. (Gen 12:10; Job 37:9; Zech 9:14; Matt 12:42; Luke 12:55.)

Space (see sky)

Spark: Source of ignition; origin; certainty; the strength of man; demonic attack; conflict; (Job 5:7; Isa 1:31; Isa 50:11; Eph 6:16.)

Sparrow (see bird)

Spider/spider web: Skillful; evil spirit; spiritual or natural poison; web of deceit; entanglement; control or manipulation; religious spirit; misplaced trust; witchcraft; sickness; sin; death. (Job 8:14; Prov 30:28; Isa 59:5.)

Spring (season): Newness; fresh start; time of war (natural or spiritual). (2 Sam 11; Job 29:23; Isa 43:19; Acts 3:19.)

Spy: Servant of God; prophet; covert collector of information; traveling or seeing in the spirit; enemy; evil spirit; traitor. (Num 13:16-17; Judg 18:2; 1 Kings 18:11-2; 2 Kings 5:25-26; 2 Kings 6:12; Gal 2:4; Luke 6:16.)

Square: Global; precise; rigid; religious; legalistic. (Ex 27:1; Lev 19:9; 1 Kings 7:31; Isa 11:12; Ezek 41:21; Rev 7:1; Rev 20:8; Rev 21:16.)

Staff: Natural or supernatural authority or power; rule; instruction; correction; support; trust; weapon; pledge; old age; infirmity; idolatry. (Gen 38:18; Judg 5:14; Judg 6:21; 1 Sam 17:7; 2 Sam 3:29; 2 Kings 4:29; 2 Kings 18:21; Isa 9:4; Isa 10:5; Isa 14:5; Isa 30:32; Hos 4:12; Mic 7:14; Zech 8:4; Zech 11:7-17; Heb 11:21.)

Stairs: Ascend; elevation; promotion; ambition; before a throne or altar; descend; fall into sin. (Gen 28:12; 1 Kings 10:19; Prov 5:5; Ezek 40:22.)

Star: Angel; Christ; Satan; Israel; innumerable; descendant; the wise; those who turn others to righteousness; fame; heavenly sign; Wormwood; idolatry. (Gen 15:5; Gen 37:9-10; Deut 4:19; Judg 5:20; Job 38:7; Isa 14:13; Isa 47:13; Dan 8:10; Dan 12:3; Matt 2:2; Matt 24:29; 2 Pet 1:19;

Jude 1:13; Rev 1:20; Rev 2:28; Rev 6:13; Rev 8:10-11; Rev 9:1; Rev 12:1-4; Rev 22:16.)

Stone: The heart; Christ; identity; Israel; the house of God; the mountain of God; the kingdom of God; the believer; the Apostle Peter; altar of sacrifice; the law; memorial; witness; weapon; foundation; permanence; precious; stillness; heavy; strength; seal; offense; accusation; punishment; hard; indifferent; idol; spiritually dead. (Gen 28:11; Gen 28:22; Gen 31:45-47; Gen 49:24; Ex 8:26; Ex 15:16; Ex 24:12; Ex 28:12; Josh 4:7; Josh 24:27; 1 Sam 17:49; 2 Sam 16:13; 1 Kings 7:10; Job 41:24; Prov 26:27; Prov 27:3; Isa 8:14; Isa 28:16; Isa 37:19; Jer 43:10; Ezek 28:14; Ezek 36:26; Ezek 40:42; Dan 2:34-35; Dan 6:17; Matt 21:42-44; Matt 27:66; Luke 19:40; Luke 20:17; Rom 9:32-33; 1 Cor 3:12; 2 Cor 3:3; 1 Pet 2:4-5; Rev 2:17.) See also rock, precious stone.

Storm: Sudden change; the fulfillment of God's word; God's power; God's voice; trial and testing; calamity, terror, or destruction; judgment. (Ps 83:15-16; Ps 107:29; Ps 148:7-8; Isa 25:4; Isa 29:6; Isa 30:30; Nah 1:3; Jonah 1:4; Mark 4:37-39; Matt 7:24-27.)

Stranger: Christ; the Holy Spirit; an angel; someone in need; a foreigner; one who is disliked; a false god; a false teacher; (Gen 31:15; Gen 37:1; Ex 2:22; Ex 12:48; Ex 22:21; Lev 23:22; Ps 69:8; Ezek 16:32; Matt 25:35-40; John 10:5; Heb 13:2.)

Stream (see river)

Street (see highway)

String (see rope)

Stump (see root)

Submarine: Underground church; not visible to the public; stealth warship; protected; operating in the deep mysteries of God's kingdom; surprise attack from an enemy. (Josh 2:4; Acts 8:39; John 8:59; 2 Kings 5:26.)

Suicide: Remorse, guilt or shame; fear; self-hatred; self-sabotage; demonic attack. (1 Sam 31:4; Judg 9:54; Matt 27:5.)

Suit: Authority; righteousness; wealth; business; glory; redeemed; formality; vanity; hypocrisy; pride; legalism. (Gen 24:53; Gen 41:42; Zech 3:3-4; James 2:2-4; 1 Pet 5:5.)

Suitcase: Travel; temporary relocation. (2 Kings 5:5)

Summer: Opportunity; harvest time; time of drought; time of preparation; fruitfulness; (Gen 8:22; Ps 32:4; Prov 10:5; Prov 30:25; Isa 28:4; Jer 8:20; Jer 40:12.)

Sun: Times and seasons; one's father; Christ; righteousness; in the open; eternal; an idol. (Gen 1:14-16; Gen 37:9-10; 2 Sam 12:12; Ps 72:17; Ps 84:11; Prov 4:18; Mal 4:2; Matt 13:43; Matt 17:2; Rev 1:16.)

Supervisor: Natural or spiritual leader; the Holy Spirit; Christ. (Ps 25:5; John 10:11; Rom 8:14; Rom 13:1.)

Supper (see meal)

Swamp: Stagnant; lacking the flow of the Spirit; habitation of evil spirits. (Job 40:15-23.)

Swan: The Holy Spirit; purity; love; grace; solitude; unclean spirit; unforeseen event (black swan). (Lev 11:18.)

Sweep: Clean; search; remove; superficial change; judgment. (Isa 28:17; Isa 14:23; Jer 46:15; Luke 15:8-9; Matt 12:44.)

Swim: Natural or spiritual exercise; living in the flow of the Spirit; operating in the gifts of the Spirit. (Isa 66:12; Ezek 47:2-9.) See also drown.

Sword: The word of God; natural or spiritual weapon; the truth; prophecy; victory; critical or hurtful words; piercing pain; division; judgment; death; (Gen 3:24; Gen 34:26; Josh 5:13; Judg 7:14; Ps 57:4; Prov 12:18;

Prov 25:18; Isa 49:2; Matt 10:34; Luke 2:35; Eph 6:17; Heb 4:12; Rev 1:16; Rev 19:15.)

··· T ···

Table: Communion; fellowship; provision or wealth of a King; something done secretly is done "under the table;" covenant. (Ex 23:25-30; 2 Sam 9:7; 1 Kings 4:27; 1 Kings 18:19; Job 36:16; Ps 23:5; Ps 78:19; Song 1:12; Ezek 39:20; Ezek 44:16; Matt 9:10; Mark 7:28; Luke 14:10; Luke 22:27-30; Rom 11:9.)

Tail: Last in rank, stature or favor; subservient; false prophet; influence. (Deut 28:13; Deut 28:44; Isa 9:14-15; Isa 19:15; Rev 12:4.)

Tank (military): Natural or spiritual weapon of warfare; offensive or defensive capability; accommodation for a small number of soldiers (team ministry); all-terrain capability; (1 Sam 14:12-14; Eph 6:11-13; 2 Cor 10:4.)

Teacher: Natural or spiritual mentor; the Holy Spirit; Christ; a false teacher. (Matt 9:11; Matt 10:24-25; Matt 23:8-10; Eph 4:11-12; Heb 5:12-14; 1 John 2:27; 2 Pet 2:1.)

Teeth: Wisdom; humility; pride; foolishness; ferocity; destruction. (Prov 25:19; Job 16:9; Prov 30:14; Dan 7:19.)

Telephone: Natural or spiritual communication; communicating with God; angelic message; demonic influence; (Gen 22:11; Gen 31:11; Gen 46:2; Ex 3:4; 1 Sam 3:4-9; Ps 4:1; Acts 9:10-12; Acts 10:13-15.)

Telescope: Viewing events in the distant future. (Dan 8:17; Isa 2:1-4; Rev 6.)

Television: Natural or supernatural communication; divine revelation (tell-a-vision); revelation of future events; thoughts of the heart; world news (whether good or bad); propaganda; mind control. (Dan 2:29; Dan 8:17; Ezek 1:1; Ezek 22:28; Zech 1:7-8; Jer 1:11; Amos 7:7-9; Lam 2:14.)

Temple: The dwelling place of God; the human heart; Solomon's temple; Herod's temple; a future temple in Israel; the heavenly temple. (1 Kings 6:9-13; Ezek 40; John 2:19-21; 1 Cor 3:16-17; 2 Cor 6:16; Rev 3:12; Rev 11:1-2.)

Ten: The law; trial and testing. (Gen 31:41; Ex 34:28; Num 14:22; Dan 1:12; Rev 2:10.)

Tent: Home (permanent or temporary); tabernacle; dwelling place of God; the human heart; the physical body. (Gen 4:20; Gen 13:12; Gen 18:1-2; Ex 35:11; Ex 39:32-33; 2 Pet 1:13-14; 1 Cor 5:1-4.)

Thief: Natural thief; a demon; Satan; a fallen angel; the day of Christ's return; an unbeliever. (John 10:1; John 10:10; Job 24:14; 1 Thess 5:2-4; Rev 16:15.)

Thirteen: Rebellion. (Gen 14:4.)

Thorn: An annoyance; opposition; hindrance; the fruit of laziness; the cares of the world; infirmity. (Num 33:55; Ps 118:12; Prov 24:30-31; Prov 22:5; Isa 7:23-25; Matt 13:22; 2 Cor 12:7.)

Three: The Godhead (Father, Son and Spirit); complete (spirit, soul and body); witness (Peter, James and John, or Spirit, water and blood). (Matt 28:19; 1 John 5:7-8; 1 Thess 5:23.)

Throne: Royalty; authority (whether good or bad); dominion; glory; power; rulership; justice; righteousness; throne of God the Father; throne of David; throne of Satan; throne of Christ; throne of the believer; throne of the Beast. (Dan 5:17-20; Dan 7:9; Isa 9:7; Isa 66:1; Eph 1:19-21; Eph 2:6; Eph 6:12; Heb 8:1; Rev 2:13; Rev 3:21; Rev 4:4; Rev 13:2; Rev 22:1.)

Thunder (see storm)

Tiger (see leopard)

Tin: Impure; of little value; sin. (Ezek 22:18.)

Tire: Generally, a vehicle symbolizes aspects of one's ministry. Features of its tires can represent the way in which the vehicle operates, e.g., flat, bald, square, wobbling, screeching or misaligned tires may indicate (symbolically) problems that need to be addressed.

Toilet (see bathroom)

Tongue: Words; language; the thoughts of the heart; one's character; prophecy (whether true or false); matters of life and death; spiritual language; praise; justice; wisdom; righteousness; thirst; flattery; ridicule; dishonesty; perversity; pride; deceit; seduction; evil; (Josh 10:21; 2 Sam 23:2; Job 6:24; Ps 5:9; Ps 12:3; Ps 37:30; Ps 39:3; Ps 51:14; Ps 109:2; Prov 6:24; Prov 18:21; Isa 57:4; Isa 59:3; Jer 23:31; Lam 4:4; Acts 2:3-4; Acts 19:6; Rev 5:9.)

Tool/tool box: Spiritual tool, e.g., deliverance, healing, prophecy; repairing broken hearts (emotional healing); repairing relationships (reconciliation); the word of God; problem solving; training and equipping the saints; tool of the enemy. (Judg 4:21; Jer 23:29; Matt 3:10; Eph 4:11-12.)

Tornado: Literal windstorm; sudden and unexpected change; dramatic work of God; the Holy Spirit; the voice of God; the glory of God; judgment; destruction; (2 Kings 2:11; Job 38:1; Ps 58:9; Ps 77:18; Prov 1:27; Prov 10:25; Jer 23:19; Ezek 1:4; Hos 8:7; Nah 1:3.)

Tow Truck: One who helps others; assistance or direction in ministry; the Holy Spirit. (John 21:6; John 21:17-18; Acts 1:4-5.)

Tractor: Ministry related to plowing, sowing and reaping, i.e., evangelism; slow but powerful ministry; breaking new ground. (Matt 13:37-38; Luke 9:62; 1 Cor 3:6-7.)

Train: The church; powerful ministry; ministry to many people; large ministry that connects small ministries together; unceasing or unstoppable work. (Matt 16:18-19; Acts 2:1-4.)

Transparent: Living openly and honestly before all; the sea of glass; the river of life. (2 Tim 2:15; James 5:16; 2 Cor 1:12; Rev 4:6; Rev 22:1.)

Trap: Warning of entrapment; deception; seduction; control or manipulation; sin. (Job 33:15-18; Prov 7; Prov 14:27; Ps 140:5.)

Treasure: A thing of natural or spiritual value; that which the heart values; the kingdom of God; God's people; God's word; God's power; divine provision; spiritual gift(s); wisdom; wealth; wickedness. (Ex 19:5; Job 23:12; Ps 119:162; Prov 2:1-6; Prov 10:2; Matt 6:19-21; Matt 13:44; Luke 6:45; 2 Cor 4:7.)

Tree: Religious or political leader; the kingdom of God; a righteous person; Christ; family lineage; the cross; Israel; the wicked. (Dan 4:20-22; Ps 1:1-3; Ps 52:8; Ps 92:12; Prov 3:18; Job 24:20; Matt 3:10; Matt 13:31-33; Gal 3:13.)

Trophy: Heavenly reward. e.g., the crown of life, the crown of rejoicing, or the crown of righteousness; victory; memorial; pride. (Gen 15:11; 1 Kings 20:11; 1 Cor 9:24-25; 2 Tim 4:81; 1 Pet 5:4; James 1:12; Rev 2:10.)

Truck/Semi: Powerful ministry; large ministry; itinerant ministry. (Act 3:1-8; Acts 13:4-6.)

Trumpet: Proclamation or announcement; prophetic declaration. (Josh 6:3-11; Hos 5:8.)

Tsunami (tidal wave): A literal tsunami; sudden move of God; large-scale unexpected change; unanticipated events of great significance; spiritual revival. (Ex 14:21-22; Ezek 47:5.)

Tunnel: Way of exit or escape; refuge or shelter; passageway; transition from one thing to another; birthing a new thing; trial or testing; judgment. (Job 28:1-19; 1 Sam 13:61; 1 Sam 22:1; 1 Kings 18:4; 1 Kings 19:9; Isa 45:2-3; Num 16:31-33.)

Twelve: Divine rule or government. (Gen 49:28; Ex 24:4; Matt 10:1; Rev 12:1-2.)

Twenty: Waiting. (Gen 31:38; Gen 31:41; 1 Sam 7:2.)

Two: Divide; witness; testimony; discern. (Gen 1:4; Gen 32:7; Deut 19:15; 2 Tim 2:15.)

··· **U** ···

UFO: Angel of God; the Holy Spirit; fallen angel; evil spirit. (Ezek 1:15-16.)

Upstairs: Nearness to heaven; the mysteries of God's kingdom; spiritual gifts; traveling into the heavens; memories; thoughts; forgotten trauma. (Acts 1:13; Acts 2:1-4; Acts 10:9-11; Rev 4:1.)

··· **V** ···

Valley: Blessing and abundance; between mountaintops; hiddenness; humility; weakness or vulnerability; trial or testing; discouragement; depression; trouble; fear; judgment; death. (1 Sam 17:3; Ps 23:4; Ps 104:10; Isa 22:7; Isa 28:1; Isa 40:4; Ezek 32:5; Ezek 37:1-2; Joel 3:12-14.)

Vampire: Fallen angel; evil spirit. (1 Pet 5:8.)

Van: Family ministry (passenger van); commercial or marketplace ministry (delivery van); courier. (Acts 8:26-29; Acts 16:31-33.)

Veil: Spiritual blindness; separation between God and man; separation between natural and spiritual; lacking understanding or discernment; the law. (Ex 34:33-35; Ex 40:3; Matt 27:51; Luke 24:45; 2 Cor 3:13-16.)

Vine: Christ; Israel; the church; the believer. (Ps 128:1-3; John 15:1-8; Luke 20:9-19; Rev 14:18-20.)

Virgin: Sexual purity; Mary, the mother of Jesus; the believer; the church; righteousness; devotion to God. (Matt 1:23; Matt 25:8-9; 1 Cor 7:25-37; 2 Cor 11:2; Rev 14:4.)

Volcano: Literal volcano; God's presence; sudden move of God; unexpected change; warning of impending danger; unresolved anger; judgment; the lake of fire. (Ex 19:18; Ex 13:21; Ps 11:6; 2 Pet 3:10-11; Rev 19:20; Rev 21:8.)

Vulture: Opportunistic; self-serving; predatory; death. (Gen 15:11; Jer 12:9.)

⋯ W ⋯

Wall: Fortification; security; protection; vantage point; partition; barrier; boundary; obstacle; restriction; the heart; misplaced trust; (Ex 14:22; Num 22:24; Deut 3:5; 1 Sam 25:16: 2 Sam 11:24; Neh 2:17; Prov 18:11; Prov 25:28; Isa 62:6; Ezek 8:7-12; Ezek 13:10-15; Nah 3:8; Zech 2:5; Eph 2:14.)

Wallet: Identity; matters of the heart; finances; that which we value; qualification; citizenship; calling; divine destiny. (Prov 2:1; Jer 1:5; Matt 6:19-21; Matt 12:35; John 12:3-6; Rom 1:1.)

Warehouse: Heaven; place of manufacturing, storage and distribution; unconventional church; training and equipping. (Acts 2:1; Acts 20:7.)

Wash: Natural or spiritual cleansing; removal of sin (redemption); renewing of the mind and spirit (being born of the Spirit); sanctification; restoration; renewal. (Ps 26:6; Ps 51:2; Isa 1:16; Jer 2:22; Matt 23:25-26; 1 Cor 6:11; Eph 5:25-27; Titus 3:5; Rev 1:15; Rev 7:14.)

Wasp: Instrument of God; evil spirit. (Ex 23:2.)

Watch: Times and seasons; strategic timing; revelation of the timing of an event; divinely ordained time; waiting on God's timing; appointment; opportunity; watchfulness. (Dan 9:2; Dan 9:24-27; Matt 24:36; 1 John 2:18; Acts 1:7.)

Water: Source of life; the Holy Spirit; the word of God; Christ; the deep mysteries of God's kingdom; the heart; God's blessing; abundance; provision; passageway; deliverance; confirmation; witness; baptism; cleansing; commerce; healing; purity; teach; nation; unstable; trouble or adversity; tears; weakness; wickedness; judgment; (Gen 7:7; Gen 13:10; Gen 21:19; Gen 49:4; Ex 14:21-22; Ex 17:6; Judg 6:38; Ps 1:3; Ps 42:7; Ps 63:1; Ps 69:2; Ps 106:11; Ps 107:23; Ps 119:136; Prov 11:25; Prov 18:4; Prov 20:5; Prov 21:1; John 4:14; James 3:11-12; Isa 44:3; Isaiah 58:11; Jer 2:13; Jer 6:7; Jer 9:1; Ezek 7:17; Ezek 36:25; Ezek 47:8; Matt 3:11; John 3:5; John 4:10-14; John 7:38; 1 Cor 3:6-8; 1 John 5:8; Rev 17:15; Rev 22:1.) See also river and sea.

Weasel: Playful; untrustworthy; evil spirit.

Web (see spider)

Wedding: Natural marriage; spiritual covenant; the church as the Bride of Christ; devotion to God; agreement; partnership (whether good or bad); bondage; idolatry. (Isa 61:10; Hos 4:13-14; Matt 22:1-13; 1 Cor 7; 2 Cor 6:14; Rev 19:6-8.)

Weed: Unfruitful thoughts or actions; the consequence of neglect; the cares of the world; sin. (Job 31:40; Zeph 2:9; Matt 13:22.)

Well: Source of life; depths of God's kingdom; the Holy Spirit; Christ; righteousness; wisdom; the believer; the church. (Ex 15:27; Prov 10:11; Prov 16:22; Prov 18:4; John 4:7-14.)

West: The end; the last; sunset; death. (Ps 50:1; Matt 24:27.)

Wheat (see seed)

Wheel: Transportation; gear; load bearing; force multiplier; steering; speed; distance; commerce; angel of God; the Holy Spirit; destruction; judgment. (1 Kings 7:30; Prov 20:26; Eccl 12:6; Isa 5:28; Ezek 1:15-16; Dan 7:9.) See also tire.

Whirlwind: A literal windstorm; sudden and unexpected change; dramatic work of God; the Holy Spirit; the voice of God; the glory of God; judgment; destruction; (2 Kings 2:11; Job 38:1; Ps 58:9; Ps 77:18; Prov 1:27; Prov 10:25; Jer 23:19; Ezek 1:4; Hos 8:7; Nah 1:3.)

White: Holy; pure; heavenly; angelic; wise; aged; light; righteous; ready for harvest; leprous (sinful); hypocrisy (whitewashed). (Num 12:10; Dan 7:9; Dan 12:10; Matt 17:2; Matt 23:27; John 4:35; John 20:12; Rev 2:17; Rev 6:2; Rev 7:14; Rev 19:11.)

Widow/widower: One whose spouse has died; suffering or grief; outcast by society but cared for by God; seeking God; humble; vulnerable. (Ex 22:22; Deut 10:18; Matt 23:14; Mark 12:43; Luke 18:1-8.)

Wife (see bride)

Wilderness (see desert)

Wind: The Holy Spirit; the breath of life; the power of God; false doctrine; unbelief; vanity; destruction; judgment. (Job 1:19; Job 6:26; Job 27:20-21; Ps 11:6; Eccl 1:14; Eph 4:14; James 1:6; Acts 2:2.)

Window: Opening to heaven; opening to the soul; vantage point through which prophetic revelation is viewed; portal to the kingdom of God; window of opportunity; escape; exposure; vulnerable. (Gen 7:11; 1 Sam 19:12; Prov 7:6-7; Ezek 8:7-9; Mal 3:10; Joel 2:9; Matt 17:1-3; Rev 4:1.)

Wine: The Holy Spirit; joy; the blood of Christ; love; communion; resurrection; blessing; wisdom; drunkenness; foolishness; confusion; idolatry; destruction; violence; judgment; death. (Gen 9:21; Gen 27:28; Ps 4:7; Ps 60:3; Ps 75:8; Ps 104:15; Prov 4:17; Prov 9:1-2; Prov 20:1; Song 1:2; Matt 9:17; Matt 11:19; 1 Tim 5:23; Rev 14:8; Rev 14:10.)

Wine skin: Vessel of the Holy Spirit, i.e., the believer or the church; (Matt 9:17.)

Wing: Refuge; protection; hiddenness; God's presence; angel (whether good or bad); strength; swiftness; escape; deliverance; healing; fleeting. (Ex 19:4; Ex 25:20; Ruth 3:9; Ps 17:8; Ps 55:6; Prov 23:5; Isa 40:31; Mal 4:2; Matt 23:37; Rev 12:14.)

Winter: Time of pruning; dormant; inactive; preparation; waiting; rainy season; trial and testing; hardship; death. (Gen 8:22; Prov 20:4; Song 2:11; Matt 24:20; Acts 27:12.)

Wolf: One who appears godly but is not; deceiver; divider; destroyer; false prophet; false teacher; evil spirit. (Gen 49:27; Jer 5:6; Ezek 22:27; Matt 7:15; Matt 10:16; John 10:11-13; Acts 20:29.)

Woman: A woman who appears in a dream or vision may represent the person they appear to be, or another person. The demeanor of the woman, her words, actions and appearance are clues to who she represents. Sometimes an old woman represents our old ways. A young woman might represent the dreamer at a young age. Other interpretations are the church; Israel; the Holy Spirit; Wisdom; an angel (whether good or bad); a mentor; a spiritual mother; the heavenly Jerusalem; a false religious system; a spirit of control; a seducing spirit. (Prov 2:16; Prov 11:22; Prov 14:1; Jer 3:1-3; Jer 6:2; Eph 5:25-27; 2 Cor 11:2; Rev 2:20; Rev 12:1-4; Rev 17:1-4; Rev 21:2.)

Wound: Physical injury; painful memory; emotional wound in need of healing. (Isa 61:1; Matt 9:12; Luke 4:18.)

··· **X** ···

X-ray: Medical examination, diagnosis and treatment; prophetic insight. (2 Chron 16:12; Jer 8:22; Ps 147:3; Ps 147:3; Luke 8:43-44.)

··· **Y** ···

Yard: A back yard speaks of that which is private; unknown; hidden; related to the past; or one's ancestry. A front yard speaks of that which is open; known to the public; related to the future; or related to one's destiny.

Yellow: Welcome; timidity; cowardliness.

CHAPTER TWENTY-THREE

Names

THIS CHAPTER IS PROVIDED AS a reference for those who wish to know the meaning of certain names. Due to space constraints, it is impossible to provide an exhaustive list of names. Many websites are available with search tools that can provide the meaning of a name not found in this chapter. There is not universal agreement on the origin and meaning of every name. In a few cases, two meanings will be provided, each one representing a different view of the name's origin. Some names have many variations. Occasionally, several variations will be provided, but when other versions exist, they all have the same meaning.

Aaron: Elevated, strong
Abigail/Abby: Joy of the father
Ace: The best
Ada: Noble
Adair: Wealthy spear

Adalia: God is my refuge
Adam: Made from the earth
Addison: Son of Adam
Adelaide/Adele: Noble, kind
Adina: Delicate
Adler: Eagle
Adrian/Adrianne: From Adria
Agatha: Virtuous
Agnes: Sacred and chaste
Ahmed: Praiseworthy
Aida: Happy
Aiden: Little fire
Ainsley: Meadow
Alan/Alana: Precious or little rock
Albert: Brilliant
Alessa: Defender
Alex/Alexander/Alexis/Alexandra: Defender of the people
Alice: Noble
Alyssa: Rational
Amber: From the precious stone
Amelia: Ambitious worker
Amira: Princess
Amy: Beloved
Anastasia: Resurrection
Andrew: Manly
Angela: Messenger of God
Angus: One strength
Anna/Anne/Anita/Anika: Graceful
Annabelle: Beauty and grace
April: Open
Aria: Lioness
Ariana: Holy
Asher: Blessed
Ashley: Ash tree field
Ashton: Ash tree town
Audra: Noble strength
Aurora: Dawn
Austin: Great
Ava: Like a bird

Avery: Elf king
Bailey: Justice officer
Baldwin: Bold friend
Barbara: Stranger
Barnard/Barney: Brave bear
Beatrice: One who brings joy
Beau: Handsome
Bella: Beautiful, God is my oath
Benjamin: Son of my right hand
Benedict/Benito: Blessed
Benson: Son of Ben
Bentley: Bent grass meadow
Bert/Bertha: Shining, bright
Bethany: Place of figs
Bethel: House of God
Betsy: God is my oath
Bianca: White
Bill/Billie: Strong-willed warrior
Bindi: A drop
Blair: Plain or field
Blake: Pale blonde one
Blanche: White, pure
Blythe: Cheerful
Bodhi: Awakened, enlightened
Bonnie: Beautiful
Braden: From the wide valley
Bram: Father of multitudes
Brigitte: Exalted
Brittany: From Great Britain
Brooke: Small stream
Brynn: Honorable
Cadence: Rhythm
Caitlin: Pure
Caleb: Whole hearted
Callum: Dove
Cameron: Bent nose
Camille/Camilla: Perfect
Candice: Queen mother
Cara/Carissa: Friend

Carl: Strong
Carlin: Little champion
Carlton: From the town of free men
Carmelo: Vineyard of the Lord
Carmen: Poem
Carol: Song
Carter: Cart maker
Casey: Brave
Cassandra: Temptress
Catherine: Pure
Cato: Good judgment, wisdom
Cecilia: Blind to one's own beauty
Celeste: Celestial, heavenly
Chandler: Candle maker
Charles/Charlotte: Free
Chase: Hunter
Cheryl: Beloved
Chloe: Green shoot
Christian: Follower of Christ
Christopher: Christ-bearer
Clark: Learned scholar
Claude: Lame
Cleo: Praise
Cleopatra: Glory of the father
Cody: Helpful
Cole: Victory of the people
Connor: Dog-lover
Constance: Unchanging
Cooper: Barrel maker
Cora: Heart, maiden
Cortez: Courteous
Cosgrove: From the cow's grove
Costa: From the coast
Covey: From the cove
Craig: From the crag (rock)
Crosby: Village by the cross
Cynthia: Luminous
Dahlia: From the flower
Daisy: From the flower

Dale: Valley
Dalton: From the valley town
Damien: To tame or subdue
Danica: Morning star
Daniel/Daniele: God is my judge
Darby: Freedom
Daria/Dario: Upholder of good
Darren: Great
David: Beloved
Dempsey: Proud
Denise: Lover of wine and revelry
Diane: Divine
Dillon: Faithful
Donna: Lady
Donovan: Dark haired
Doris: Sea
Duncan: Dark skinned warrior
Dylan: Son of the sea
Earl: Nobleman, prince
Eden: Paradise
Edmond/Edward: Wealthy protector
Edna: Pleasant
Edwin: Wealthy friend
Elaine/Eleanor/Elena: Light
Eli: High
Eliana: God has answered
Elijah/Elias: The Lord is my God
Elizabeth/Elsa: God is my oath
Ella: Young Girl
Ellie: Noble
Eloi: Chosen
Eloise: Famous warrior
Emery: Industrious
Emily/Emilia: To strive, excel or rival
Emma: Universal
Eric: Always ruler
Esmé: Beloved
Esmeralda: Emerald
Estelle: Star

Ethan: Firm, strong
Eva: Giver of Life
Evelyn: Beautiful bird
Everly: Boar meadow
Ezra: Help
Faith: Faith
Fatima: Daughter of the prophet
Felix: Happy and prosperous
Fidel: Faithful
Finley: Fair haired warrior
Finn: Fair
Flynn: Descendant of the red-haired man
Frances/Francesca: Free one
Gabriel/Gabrielle: God is my strength
Genesis: Beginning
George/Georgia: Farmer
Gianna: God is gracious
Glen: From the valley
Gloria: Glory
Grace: Grace of God
Grady: Noble, renowned
Grant: Tall, great
Grayson: Son of the gray-haired man
Greta: A pearl
Guy: Forest
Haley: Hay meadow
Hamish: Supplanter
Hannah: Grace
Harper: Harp player
Harriet: Home ruler
Harrison: Son of Harry
Harry: Army ruler
Hayden/Hayley/Hailey: From the hay clearing
Hazel: The hazel tree
Heidi: Noble
Hella: The sun's rays
Henry: Ruler of the house
Hera: Queen, protector
Herbert: Brilliant warrior

Hermes: Messenger
Hilda: Woman warrior
Hillary: Cheerful
Hillel: Greatly praised
Holly: Plant with red berries
Horace: Time keeper
Howard: Watcher, guardian
Howell: Eminent
Hubert/Hugh: Bright mind and heart
Hudson: Son of Hudd
Humbert: Renowned warrior
Humphrey: Peaceful warrior
Hunter: One who hunts
Ida: Hardworking
Ike: He will laugh
Imogen: Innocent, girl
Ingrid: Ing's beauty
Ira: Watchful
Irene: Peace
Iris: Rainbow
Isaac: Laughter
Isabel/Isabella: God is my oath
Isadora: Gift of Isis
Isaiah: God is salvation
Isla: Island
Ivy: From the plant
Jabbar: Powerful
Jack: God is gracious
Jackson/Jaxon/Jax: Son of Jack
Jacob/Jake: Supplanter
Jade: Green gemstone
Jamal: Handsome
James/Jamie: Supplanter
Jasmine: From the flower
Jason/Jayson/Jayce: Healer
Jay: Blue crested bird
Jayden/Jaiden/Jaden: God has heard
Jaylan: Calm
Jeffery: Man of peace

Jennifer: Fair lady
Jesse: The Lord exists
Jessica: God beholds
Joel: Jehovah is the Lord
John: God is gracious
Jolie: Pretty
Jonah: Dove
Jordan: To flow down
Joseph: God will increase
Joshua: God is my salvation
Josiah: God will save
Joy: Joy
Jude: Praised
Julian: Youthful
Justin: Righteous, just
Kacy/Kacey: Vigilant
Kade: From the wetlands
Kadir: Capable
Kai: Ocean
Kalani: The heavens
Kalliope: Beautiful voice
Kamala: Lotus flower
Kara: Dear
Karen: Pure
Katherine/Kate/Katelyn/Katrina/Kayla: Pure
Keanu: Mountain breeze
Keira: Dark
Kendra/Kendal: Ruler of the valley
Kent: High, coastal land
Kin: Golden
Kingsley: From the king's meadow
Kingston: From the king's town
Kirby: Town by a church
Kristin: Christian
Kyle: Channel, strait
Kyra: Lady
Lachlan: From the land of lakes
Lala: Tulip
Lamar: From the sea

Lana: Light
Lauren: Laurel
Laverne: Alder tree
Layla: Night, black
Leah: Weary
Leandra/Leo/Leon: Lion man
Leif: Beloved
Leonard: Brave as a lion
Leroy: King
Levi: Joined in harmony
Liam: Strong-willed warrior
Lilly: From the flower
Lincoln: Lake colony
Logan: From the hollow
Lola: Sorrows
Louis: Famed warrior
Lucas/Luca/Luke: From Lucania, Italy
Lucy: Light
Luna: The moon
Mackenzie: Son of Kenneth
Madeline: Woman of Magdala
Madison: Son of Matthew
Maia: Great
Marcus: Warlike
Maren: Pearl of the sea
Maria/Marion: Sea of bitterness
Marlow: From the hill by the lake
Martha: Lady
Mason: Stone worker
Mateo: Gift of God
Matilda: Battle strength
Matthew: Gift of God
Maverick: Independent
Max: Greatest
Maya: Dream or illusion
Mia: Sea of bitterness
Michael/Michelle: Who is like God?
Mila: People's favor
Mildred/Mille: Gentle strength

Miller: Mill worker
Milo: Soldier, merciful
Mirabelle: Wondrous
Molly: Sea of bitterness
Mona: Desires, wishes
Muhammad: Praised
Nadia: Hope
Natalie: Born on Christmas day
Nathan: He gave
Nicholas/Nicole: Victory of the people
Nina: Little girl
Noah: Rest
Noel: Christmas
Nora: Honor
Norman: From the north
Nova: New
Oakley: Oak tree meadow
Odele: Wealth
Oliver/Olivia: Olive tree
Ophelia: Helper
Oscar: Deer lover
Otis: Wealth
Otto: Wealth
Owen: Yew tree, youth
Paco: Free
Paige: Assistant
Paisley: Church
Patricia: Noble, aristocrat
Paul: Small
Penelope: Weaver
Philadelphia: Brotherly love
Phoebe: Bright, shining
Phoenix: Blood red
Poppy: The flower
Rafi: Exalted
Raleigh: Deer's meadow
Ralph: Wolf counsel
Randall/Randy: Wolf shield
Raphael: God has healed

Ravi: Sun
Rebecca: To bind
Renee: Reborn
Reuben: Behold, a son
Richard: Brave ruler
Riley: Rye clearing
Rio: River
Rita: Pearl
Roan: Red-haired
Robert: Bright fame
Robson/Robertson: Son of Robert
Rocco: Rest
Roger: Famous spear
Roland: Famous land
Roman: from Rome, Italy
Ronan: Little seal
Rose: From the flower
Roxanne: Dawn
Ruby: Red gemstone
Ryan: King
Sadie: Princess
Sally: Princess
Samuel/Samantha: His name is God
Sandra: Defender of the people
Sarah: Princess
Savannah: Open plain
Scarlett: Red
Schneider: Tailor
Seamus: Supplanter
Sebastian: Honorable
Serge/Sergio: Servant
Seth: Appointed
Sienna: Reddish brown
Sofia/Sophia: Wisdom
Solange: Solemn
Stella: Star
Taylor: Tailor
Tessa: Harvester
Thomas: A twin

Tobias/Toby: God is good
Tristan: Tumult
Troy: Foot soldier
Tyler: Tile maker
Tyson: Firebrand
Valerie: Strength
Venus: Love
Vera: Faith
Vincent/Victor/Victoria: Victory
Violet/Viola: From the flower
Virginia: Virgin, pure
Vito: Life
Vivienne: Alive
William: Strong-willed warrior
Willow: From the willow tree
Wyatt: Son of Guy
Xavier: The new house
Xena: Hospitable
Yasmine: From the jasmine flower
Zachary: God has remembered
Zadie: Princess
Zelda: Dark battle
Zion: Israel
Zoe: Life
Zola: Earth

INKITY
PRESS™

Other books from Praying Medic

For up-to-date titles go to: PrayingMedic.com

Series—The Kingdom of God Made Simple:

Divine Healing Made Simple
Seeing in the Spirit Made Simple
Hearing God's Voice Made Simple
Traveling in the Spirit Made Simple

Series—My Craziest Adventures with God:

My Craziest Adventures with God - Volume 1
My Craziest Adventures with God - Volume 2

Series—The Courts of Heaven:

Defeating Your Adversary in the Court of Heaven
Operating in the Court of Angels

And more:

Emotional Healing in 3 Easy Steps
The Gates of Shiloh (a novel)
God Speaks: Perspectives on Hearing God's Voice (28 authors)
A Kingdom View of Economic Collapse (eBook only)
American Sniper: Lessons in Spiritual Warfare (eBook only)

SCAN THIS TO GO TO
PrayingMedic.com ▶

Printed in the USA
CPSIA information can be obtained
at www.ICGtesting.com
CBHW062349271223
3004CB00008B/633